CW00762273

DOS
Problem Solver

William Barden, Jr.

Scott, Foresman and Company
Glenview, Illinois   London

Library of Congress Cataloging-in-Publication Data

Barden, William T.
    DOS problem solver / William Barden, Jr.
        p.   cm. -- (Problem solver series)
ISBN 0-673-46145-9
    1. DOS 4 (Computer operating system). 2. PC DOS
(Computer operating sys;tem)
    I. Title. II. Series
QA76.76.063B365 1989
005.4'469--dc20   89-10883
                                        CIP

    1 2 3 4 5 6 EBI 94 93 92 91 90 89

ISBN 0-673-46145-9

Notice of Liability

Scott, Foresman professional books are available for bulk
sales at quantity discounts. For information, please contact
Marketing Manager, Professional Books Group, Scott,
Foresman and Company, 1900 East Lake Avenue, Glenview, IL 60025.

Foreword

by Ralph Blodgett

The **Problem Solver** book in your hands represents a new concept in computer book publishing. Rather than listing features of a program one after another, this series of books offers—in a quickly accessible format—answers to typical problems that users encounter when using a particular piece of software.

We designed the series as reference guides that you will want to keep next to your computer for quick inspection. Inside you will find brief, concise answers to 100—150 real-life problems that thousands of others before you have encountered. All of the answers are found on one, or at most two, pages.

When you encounter a problem, use this book to quickly find a solution. Let it be your resource guide to get you out of sticky situations that other books fail to warn about. In fact, if you are a beginner or intermediate user, this book will fill an important gap left by your manual and other books on the market.

Other books in the **Problem Solver** series include:

- dBase IV Problem Solver
- Excel Problem Solver
- Microsoft Word Problem Solver
- PageMaker Problem Solver
- Sprint Problem Solver
- WordPerfect Problem Solver
- Ventura Problem Solver

Acknowledgments

I would like to thank the following people for their help in planning, designing, editing, and producing this series of books:

Amy Davis, acquisitions editor for Scott, Foresman and Company, for her openness to new ideas and encouragement throughout the many, many steps necessary to create and produce this new series of books. Without her willingness to innovate and try new things, this series could not have been produced.

Joan Sandlin, of Omnicomm Publications, who copy edited all the manuscripts and provided valuable assistance to all the writers with her comments and suggestions for improvements.

William B. Sanders, of Sandlight Publications, who designed and prepared the camera ready copy for all the books in the series. I know he faced a formidable task working with 8 different authors, each with their own favorite word processing software and unique writing styles.

Diane Beausoleil and Sybil Sosin of Scott, Foresman and Company for their valuable assistance in the production of this series.

Ralph Blodgett
Series Editor

Table of Contents

Trademarks

The following terms mentioned in this book are trademarks of manufacturers:

International Business Machines Corporation: IBM, IBM PC, PC-XT, PC AT, PS/2 series, Proprinter

Microsoft Corporation: MS-DOS 3.3, MS DOS 4.0, MS-DOS 4.01, Microsoft Windows, Microsoft Mouse

Lotus Development Corporation: Lotus 1-2-3

Borland International: Sidekick

Fifth Generation Systems, Inc: Fastback

Intel Corporation: Intel Above Board Plus

Peter Norton Computing, Inc.: Norton Utilities

Central Point Software: PC Tools

Apple Computer: Apple IIGS

Hewlett-Packard Company: LaserJet, LaserJet Series II

Introduction

Do you have a question about DOS 4.0? Our goal is to provide quick and easy reference to some of the most commonly asked questions you might have. This book is meant to be a ready helpmate for the beginner as well as a reference you can also use as you gain experience and knowledge of DOS.

Each new version of IBM PC-DOS and Microsoft MS-DOS has built on preceding versions to add more and more capability. DOS 4.0 is no exception. DOS 4.0 adds a graphics display that makes navigating around the operating system much easier for newcomers to computers, while adding a great deal more versatility for even more experienced users. It adds expanded memory capability to handle system memories above the previous 640K byte limit. It adds the ability to use hard disks greater than 32M bytes in size. In addition, many new commands have been added that simplify file manipulation and operating systems functions. Also, old commands have been enhanced and error messages made more meaningful.

The DOS 4.0 Problem Solver anticipates some of the questions that beginners to DOS and intermediate users may have about this new version of DOS: How can I add a mouse?; What's the meaning of "File not found"; Why does my printer print garbage characters? It is divided into eleven sections, each one concerned with a major area of interest: Batch Files and PSCs,

Displays, Files, Floppy Disks, Hard Disks, Mouse, Operations, Printers, Programs, Startup, and Utilities. Within each section questions are alphabetized for easy reference. A short glossary follows. It can help beginners decipher the jargon of DOS terms. A comprehensive index lists topics in more detailed form.

This book is intended to cover both PC-DOS 4.0 and MS-DOS 4.0. The former is the operating system provided for IBM systems such as the IBM PC, PC-XT, PC-AT, and PS/2 series. The latter is the operating system used for PC compatibles, which are those systems that operate the same as IBM systems but built by Compaq, Epson, Hewlett-Packard, Tandy, and many others. There may be minor differences between PC-DOS and MS-DOS, but for the most part the operating systems are virtually identical. We'll use the general term "DOS" to cover both operating systems and use the more specific terms "PC-DOS" and "MS-DOS" when appropriate.

The book also applies to future releases of DOS 4.0. At this time of writing there is a DOS 4.01, which supersedes DOS 4.0. Future releases that fix minor errors will undoubtedly be labeled DOS 4.02 or perhaps DOS 4.1 and DOS 4.2. Although this book may not apply as well to a major upgrade to a DOS 5. X version, it should serve very well for any DOS 4.X versions. To make things less complicated, we'll use the generic term "DOS 4.0" instead of specific version numbers, except when absolutely necessary.

Chapter 1

Batch Files and PSCs

Batch Files and PSCs, Audio Signal

Batch files provide a lot of options, but there isn't one for an audio signal. I'd like to use such a command to signal a condition in a batch file such as a nonexistent file. How can I do this?

There's an easy way to do this in a batch file. Do a:

```
C:\>copy con: beep
^G^Z
```

The ^G character is entered by pressing the Ctrl key followed by the G key. The ^Z character is the normal end of file created by pressing the Ctrl key followed by the Z key. This sequence creates a file called BEEP consisting of the single character "Ctrl G." This is not a printable character, but is rather a "control code" character with a value of 7. (This control code was originally used to sound a bell on a teletypewriter and actually is called BEL.)

After creating the BEEP file, include

```
type beep
```

in any batch file to get an audio signal.

To make life easier, I'm using many different batch files, both in DOS SHELL and command prompt mode. However, I'm getting confused about which is which. Is there any way to put comments in the batch files?

Yes, an easy way. *Labels* can be used within batch files to mark places to which a batch GOTO command transfers control. A label is any 8-character string preceded by a colon. There's no rule against using a label which is never referenced by a GOTO, and you can therefore use a line such as the following:

```
:This is a comment. It never shows
when the batch file executes.
```

As the comment indicates, labels never display on the screen during batch file execution.

I want to use a batch file in command prompt mode to instruct a computer operator to insert a data disk in drive A: before continuing. How do I do it?

The key here is use of ECHO, PAUSE, and IF NOT EXIST. Here's a sample of what you might use:

```
@ECHO off
ECHO Put DATA DISK#1 in drive A:
ECHO Make certain the diskette
    label is up and the door shut
PAUSE
IF NOT EXIST A:REPTPROG.EXE ECHO
    *****TRY AGAIN*****
IF EXIST A:REPTPROG.EXE A:REPTPROG
```

ECHO displays any text after "ECHO". The @ character before the first ECHO makes certain the ECHO is not displayed before ECHO OFF turns off display of batch commands.

The PAUSE displays the message "Press any key to continue" and pauses until the user presses a key.

The IF NOT EXIST tests whether file A:REPTPROG.EXE is present on the diskette in A:. If not, the "*****TRY AGAIN*****" message is displayed; otherwise the program is run.

The display output is:

Put DATA DISK#1 in drive A: Make Certain the
diskette label is up and the door shut
Press any key to continue
. . . (program starts)

You can use this approach to enter any
number of instructions. See "Files, Short ASCII"
and "Batch Files and PSCs, Simple PSC User
Instructions. "

Batch Files and PSCs, Simple PSC User Instructions

I want to use a set of PSCs to instruct a computer operator to insert a data disk in drive A: before continuing. How do I do it?

The key here is use of PSC options. Options must be enclosed in brackets. Here's a sample of what might be entered in the Commands field for the Program:

```
/I "Put DATA DISK#1 in drive A:"
/F"A:REPTPROG.EXE" A:REPTPROG
```

These are entered as a single long string:

```
[/I"Put DATA DISK#1 in drive A:"/
F"a:reptprog.exe"]| a:reptprog
```

The first /I option defines a prompt line that is displayed before the program is executed. After the prompt is displayed, DOS asks for program parameters. In this case there are none, so <ENTER> is pressed. Next DOS checks the existence of file A:REPTPROG.EXE on disk drive A:. If the file doesn't exist on drive A:, a beep sounds and the sequence repeats. Using this series of Program Startup Commands, therefore, allows you to start the program only if the program file is present in drive A:.

You can use this approach to enter a number of instructions. See "Files, Short ASCII."

You also can substitute an existing batch file for a set of PSC commands. See "Batch Files and PSCs, Using Existing Batch Files. "

I'm now using DOS 4.0 with the SHELL, but have a number of batch files for automatic loading and execution of programs. How do I use these with DOS SHELL PSCs?

It's easy to incorporate an existing batch file with Program Startup Commands. Suppose you have a batch file called REPORT.BAT:

```
@ECHO off
ECHO Put DATA DISK#1 in drive A:
ECHO Make certain the diskette label
   is up and the door shut
PAUSE
IF NOT EXIST A:REPTPROG.EXE ECHO
   *****TRY AGAIN*****
IF EXIST A:REPTPROG.EXE A:REPTPROG
```

This batch file displays a series of messages to tell the user to put the proper diskette in drive A: before proceeding, and then starts program REPTPROG.EXE in drive A:.

To execute this batch file, you'd need to enter the following PSCs in the Commands field for Program:

```
call report.bat
```

And that's it! The batch file would execute as it does normally, not under the DOS SHELL, but as if it were in command prompt mode. However, at the end of the program execution, return is made to the DOS SHELL.

What are batch files and how can they be used?

A batch file is nothing more than a sequence of DOS commands put together in a single text file. The file can be created by your word processor, EDLIN, or a COPY command (see "Files, Short ASCII"). Suppose that you needed to perform the following operations in command prompt mode:

```
C:\>cd c:\sprint\text
C:\>dir
C:\>cd c:\
```

This short sequence simply changes the current directory to subdirectory C:\SPRINT\TEXT, lists the directory, and then changes the current directory back to the root.

The same commands could be used in the file CHECKDIR.BAT:

```
cd c:\sprint\text
dir
cd c:\
```

This is a three-line text file which now can be run by entering the batch file name CHECKDIR.BAT in command prompt mode:

```
C:\>checkdir
```

The extension .BAT is not necessary here, as

DOS assumes the extension on such a name is either .BAT , .COM , or .EXE. The result is as if the three commands have been entered manually.

Batch files, in essence, are an automatic way to store and later execute a list of DOS commands. Batch files also can be used in Program Startup Commands (see "Batch Files and PSCs, Using Existing Batch Files").

What are PSCs and how can they be used?

PSC stands for Program Startup Command. It is the DOS SHELL version of a batch file. Each program in a group can have a list of startup commands that aid in starting the program by issuing instructions to an operator, checking for the existence of a file, and so forth. In the simplest case, only one PSC is used - the actual name of the program to be run. Suppose that you needed to perform the following operations to start program RPTPRGM1.EXE, located in directory C:\INVOICE\PROGRAMS:

```
C:\>cd c:\invoice\programs
C:\>rptprgm1
```

This short sequence simply changes the current directory to subdirectory C:\INVOICE\PROGRAMS and then starts program RPTPRGM1.EXE.

The Program Startup Commands for doing this are added to the Commands field in the Add Program screen for DOS SHELL. The actual line added is:

```
cd c:\invoice\programs|rptprgm1
```

The double line between the commands is entered by pressing the F4 key. When this program is selected from the Start Programs screen in DOS SHELL, the two commands will be executed automatically.

This is a very simple case of PSCs, but many programs need be no more complicated than this. More complicated startup procedures can be done by adding more PSCs. There are more examples in this "Batch File and PSCs" section.

I'm confused. When should Program Startup Commands be used, and when should Batch Files be used to run programs?

It all depends upon how you operate. If you do a great many operations from the DOS SHELL, then it's probably advantageous to use PSCs whenever possible. PSCs allow you to use simple start up commands easily before a file is actually run. Just about every thing that can be done pertaining to program execution can be done in PSCs as well as batch files.

Batch files, on the other hand, can be run from PSCs as well (see "Batch Files and PSCs, Using Existing Batch Files"), so you can have the best of both worlds. You also can also enter batch commands as PSCs (except for GOTO commands).

When it comes to performing tricks with batch files other than program execution, however, batch files offer a good deal more flexibility. They are a mini programming language with the ability to alter the sequence of execution by GOTO commands and labels. The GOTO command, however, will *not* run from within a PSC format. Learning batch techniques, though, is like learning any programming language; it's somewhat tedious and more difficult than working with PSCs.

I'd like to use batch files to do such operations as DISKCOPY. However, DISKCOPY requires a Y or N (yes or no) response. How can I provide this automatically?

This problem is similar to the one described under "Operations, Redirecting Input. " The yes or no response consists of a single character. The single characters can be put into files called YES and NO. A COPY CON: command in command prompt mode does this simply:

```
C:\>copy con: yes
Y^Z
```

The ^Z in the above file is entered by pressing the Ctrl key followed by the Z key. The result is a single character file of Y or N. This file is then specified as the input file for a DISKCOPY operation by the < character. Assuming there are no gross errors there is only one usual input: a Y or N.

```
diskcopy a: b: <no
```

The line above can be used in a batch file for automatic copying (with the exception of actually placing the diskette in the drive, that is). The Y or N files also can be used for any other file requiring a yes or no response.

Chapter 2

Displays

Displays, Changing

I have a VGA (or EGA) display, but at times would like to see the DOS SHELL menus displayed in text mode. How can I do this?

The DOS SHELL displays probably are being set automatically as the startup options in the DOSSHELL.BAT file. You can change the mode from VGA or EGA to text mode easily by creating a new DOSSHELL.BAT file with the name of your choice. As an example, let's assume that DOSSHELL.BAT is in the root directory of drive C:. You want to create a new DOS SHELL file called DOSSHTXT.BAT. COPY the DOSSHELL.BAT to a new file DOSSHTXT.BAT. Then modify DOSSHTXT.BAT by your word processing program or EDLIN so that the /TEXT option is used in place of /CO1, /CO2, or /CO3. If there is no present option for modes /CO1 through /CO3, simply add /TEXT to the line. In this example, you might have:

```
@SHELLC  /TEXT/COLOR/TRAN/DOS/MENU/
   MUL/SND/MEU:SHELL.MEU  CLR:SHELL
    .CLR/PROMPT/MAINT/EXIT/SWAP/DATE
```

To execute the text mode DOS SHELL at any time, exit the DOSSHELL, change the directory to C:/, and enter:

```
C:>DOSSHTXT
```

You may use any number of shells with different options by this method.

I want to change the colors in DOS SHELL, but I get the error message "This shell function is not active." What's wrong?

You have not included the /COLOR option in the startup options for the DOS SHELL. The startup options are in a line of the DOSSHELL.BAT file, normally located in C:\. Here's a typical startup line:

```
@SHELLC /COLOR/TRAN/DOS/MENU/MUL/
SND/MEU:SHELL.MEU/CLR:SHELL.CLR/
PROMPT/MAINT/EXIT/SWAP/DATE
```

Edit the DOSSHELL.BAT file and include the /COLOR option.

This error message also occurs when you attempt to do an Exit Shell without the /EXIT option or a Group function without the /MAINT option. Normally these options would be included in the startup line.

Displays, EGA Not Present

I just added an EGA controller and monitor, but the DOS displays are still in CGA (text) mode? How can I get an EGA display?

The SELECT program during DOS installation should automatically select the highest display mode that your system is capable of supporting. Make certain that the EGA controller jumper blocks or DIP switches have been properly set according to the manufacturer's directions; DOS reads display information from the system hardware. You now can rerun the INSTALL program. During the INSTALL procedure, the SELECT portion of the installation should provide you with the proper graphics option choice.

If EGA graphics is not enabled after the installation, include the /CO1 startup option in the DOSSHELL.BAT file (see "Displays, Changing" for instructions on how to include the modified command). Here is a typical startup line with the /CO1 option:

```
@SHELLC /MOS:PCMSDRV.MOS/CO1/COLOR/
TRAN/DOS/MENU/MUL/SND/MEU:SHELL.
MEU/CLR:SHELL.CLR/PROMPT/MAINT/
EXIT/SWAP/DATE
```

The /CO1 option selects EGA (640 by 350 resolution) graphics. After rebooting the system, you should see EGA graphics displayed.

You will see small icons (figures) in place of text graphics for a File System display (see Figure 1).

If DOS does not recognize the EGA graphics, the error message,

```
Display in graphics not successful
```

is displayed. Recheck your hardware jumper block and/or DIP switch settings and call the EGA controller manufacturer support line if available.

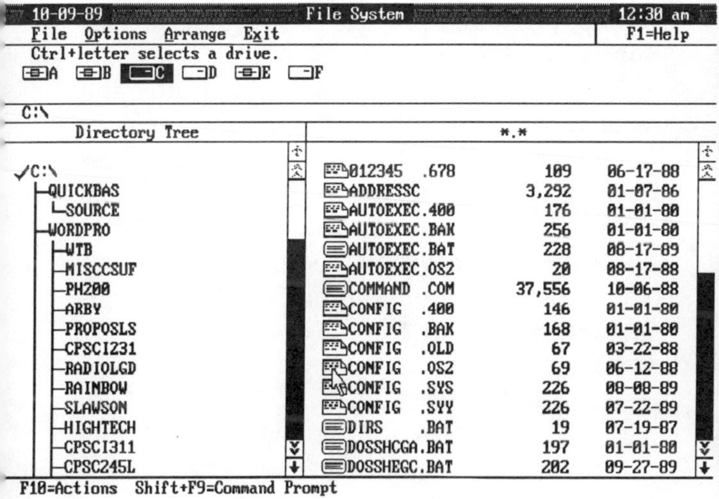

Figure 1

I just added a VGA controller and monitor, but the DOS displays are still in CGA (text) mode? How can I get a VGA display?

The SELECT program during DOS installation should automatically select the highest display mode that your system is capable of supporting. Make certain that the VGA controller jumper blocks or DIP switches have been properly set according to the manufacturer's directions, because DOS reads display information from the system hardware. You now can rerun the INSTALL program. During the INSTALL procedure, the SELECT portion of the installation should provide you with the proper graphics option choice.

If VGA graphics is not enabled after the installation, include the /CO2 or /CO3 startup options in the DOSSHELL.BAT file (see "Displays, Changing" for instructions on how to include the modified command). Option /CO2 selects two-color VGA mode, while option /CO3 selects 16-color VGA mode. Here is a typical startup line with the /CO3 option:

```
@SHELLC /MOS:PCMSDRV.MOS/CO3/COLOR/
TRAN/DOS/MENU/MUL/SND/MEU:SHELL.MEU
/CLR:SHELL.CLR/PROMPT/MAINT/EXIT/
SWAP/DATE
```

The /CO2 and /CO3 options select VGA

(640 by 480 resolution) graphics. After rebooting the system, you should see VGA graphics displayed. You will see small icons (figures) in place of text graphics in File System mode (see Figure 2).

If DOS does not recognize the VGA graphics, the error message

```
Display in graphics not successful
```

is displayed. Recheck your hardware jumper block and/or DIP switch settings and call the VGA controller manufacturer support line, if available.

```
 12:01:89                          File System                    1:00 pm
 File  Options  Arrange  Exit                                   F1=Help
 Ctrl+letter selects a drive.
 ⊟A   ⊟B  ▣C  ⊟D  ⊟E  ⊟F
─────────────────────────────────────────────────────────────────────
 C:\
      Directory Tree                              *.*
                                   ┌─────────────────────────────────
 ✓C:\                              📄012345  .678       109   06-17-88
  ├QUICKBAS                        📄ADDRESSC         3,292   01-07-86
  │ └SOURCE                        📄AUTOEXEC.400       176   01-01-80
  ├WORDPRO                         📄AUTOEXEC.BAK       256   01-01-80
  │ ├WTB                           📄AUTOEXEC.BAT       228   08-17-89
  │ ├MISCCSUF         ⬉           📄AUTOEXEC.OS2        20   08-17-88
  │ ├PH200                         📄COMMAND .COM    37,556   10-06-88
  │ ├ARBY                          📄CONFIG  .400       146   01-01-80
  │ ├PROPOSLS                      📄CONFIG  .BAK       168   01-01-80
  │ ├CPSCI231                      📄CONFIG  .OLD        67   03-22-88
  │ ├RADIOLGD                      📄CONFIG  .OS2        69   06-12-88
  │ ├RAINBOW                       📄CONFIG  .SYS       226   08-08-89
  │ ├SLAWSON                       📄CONFIG  .SYY       226   07-22-89
  │ ├HIGHTECH                      📄DIRS    .BAT        19   07-19-87
  │ ├CPSCI311                      📄DOSSHCGA.BAT       197   01-01-80
  │ ├CPSC245L                      📄DOSSHEGC.BAT       202   09-27-89
  │ ├VALLEYWA                      📄DOSSHELL.BAK       193   01-01-80
  │ ├PRNTMAST                      📄DOSSHELL.BAT       218   07-06-89
  │ ├LASER                         📄DOSSHUGB.BAT       196   08-23-89
  │ ├CPSC412                       📄DRIVER  .SYS     5,274   06-17-88
  │ └BANTAM                        📄GMOUSE  .COM     9,940   08-30-88
─────────────────────────────────────────────────────────────────────
 F10=Actions  Shift+F9=Command Prompt
```

Figure 2

Chapter 3

Files

Files, Appending Text

How can I append one file onto another in DOS?

The COPY command in command prompt mode allows you to append any number of files into a single large file. Just use the + sign between files. The files normally should be text files, although certain other types of files can be combined. Here's an example:

```
C:\>copy file1.txt+file2.txt+
file3.txt+file4.txt
```

In this case files FILE1.TXT, FILE2.TXT,

FILE3.TXT, and FILE4.TXT are combined in that order and replace file FILE1.TXT. Files FILE2.TXT, FILE3.TXT, and FILE4.TXT remain unchanged.

If you want to create a new file, include a destination file name as well. In this example, a new file B:\FILE5.TXT is created and the other four files remain unchanged:

```
C:\>copy file1.txt+file2.txt+
   file3.txt+file4.txt b:\file5.txt
```

What is the archive bit of a file, and how is it used?

Each file has an archive attribute associated with it. The archive attribute indicates to DOS whether or not the file has been backed up by BACKUP, XCOPY, or another manufacturer's backup procedure. This allows an *incremental* backup where only files that have not been previously backed up are saved on a backup diskette. At times, you might want to reset this archive attribute. For example, if you're doing an incremental type of backup and are not certain that you have a copy of several files, you may want to reset the archive attributes just to make certain they are saved on the next backup.

To change the archive attribute from the DOS SHELL, select one or more files from the File display and then choose the Change Attribute item from the File menu. Select option 2 to change all files. As files are displayed, you can see whether or not the archive attribute is on by a small triangle to the left of the text. If you wish to reset this attribute, highlight Archive in the Hidden, Read-Only, Archive menu by the arrow keys and press the space bar to reset the archive attribute (you'll see the triangle disappear). See Figure 3. Now press <ENTER> to make the change. DOS will reset the archive bit for all files selected.

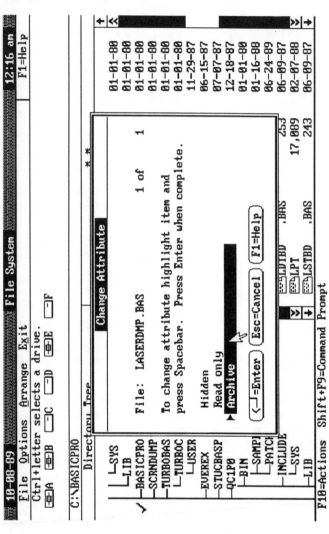

Figure 3

26

Is there an efficient way of copying and updating several dozen files? The process of selecting files and answering whether or not individual files should be deleted if they already exist on the target diskette takes a great deal of time.

Use the two "wild card" characters * and ? in the Display option in the SHELL to list *only* those files you wish to copy. The ? character denotes a single character in a file name. The * character denotes from one to eight characters. If the files to be copied have similar names, such as ACCT001.TXT, ACT002.TXT, and ACT099.TXT, you can define a generic name such as ACCT???.TXT. Only those files matching the name will then be listed.

Once the files have been listed, Select all if all are to be copied, or Select individually. Now disable the Confirm on Replace from Options. This inhibits the SHELL from asking whether each file is to be overwritten for those that already exist on the target diskette. All selected files will simply be copied without your intervention.

The fastest copy is in command prompt mode with the COPY command and a wild card name. To copy all files of the form ACCT???.* from subdirectory ACCOUNTS to subdirectory BACK1, do:

```
C:\>copy c:\accounts\acct???.*
   c:\back1\*.*
```

27

Files, Copying Over Several Diskettes

How can I copy files that total several megabytes when my 3.5-inch diskettes hold 720K? Is it okay to use several diskettes?

Yes, the copy can be done to several diskettes. List all the files you wish to copy in the DOS SHELL Display mode. Starting with a newly formatted 3.5-inch diskette, select the Copy function under files. The copy will proceed until the first 3.5-inch diskette fills up. At that point DOS will display "Disk is full." and offer the alternative of "2. Try this file or directory again."

Remove the first diskette and insert a second, formatted diskette. Select alternative 2 and the copy will proceed. This can be done as many times as necessary to copy a large amount of data onto many diskettes.

The resulting diskettes each will hold an integral number of files. The space remaining on each diskette will depend upon which file was to be written when space ran out. If the file to be written was several hundred thousand bytes, there will be up to those several hundred thousand bytes unused on the diskette.

Whenever I have to delete a significant number of files, say, twenty or thirty, it takes a great deal of time. I have to select each file to be deleted and then answer whether or not each individual file should be deleted. Isn't there an easier way?

Use the two "wild card" characters * and ? in the Display option in the SHELL to list *only* those files you wish to have deleted. See Figure 4 for a typical example. The ? character denotes a single character in a file name. The * character denotes from one to eight characters. If the files to be deleted have similar names, such as ACCT001.TXT, ACT002.TXT, and ACT099.TXT, you can define a generic name such as ACCT???.TXT. Only those files matching the name will then be listed. Of course, this is not possible in all cases.

Once the files have been listed, Select all if all are to be deleted, or Select individually.

Now disable the Confirm on Delete from Options. This inhibits the SHELL from asking whether each file is to be deleted. All selected files will simply be deleted on Delete.

The fastest delete is in command prompt mode with the DEL command and a wild card name. To delete all files of the form ACCT???.* from subdirectory ACCOUNTS, for example, do:

```
C:\>del c:\accounts\acct???.*
```

29

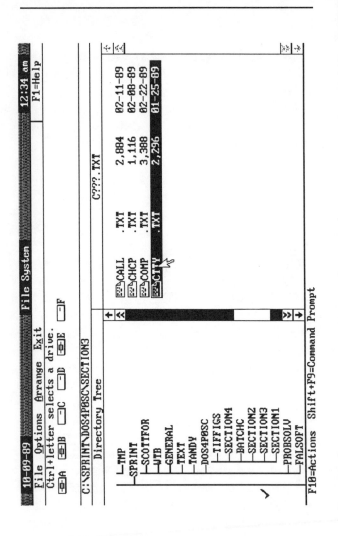

Figure 4

30

I want to display a file on the screen, but the file is displayed so rapidly that I can't see what's in it.

You can use several options to display a file a screen at a time. Under the shell, select the File System by highlighting File and then pressing <ENTER>. Using the tab key, select the file list and then select the file you want to display by using the up and down arrows. Press the space bar to select the file you want to view. Press F10 to get back to the action bar and then press <ENTER>. Use the down arrow key to highlight View, and then press <ENTER>. The file you've chosen will be displayed. Press F9 to view the file in hexadecimal, and press it again to revert to text. Use the PgDn and PgUp keys to move up and down in the file.

If you're in the command prompt mode, view a file by:

```
C:\>type filea.dat | more
```

This command will send the file to the MORE program, which displays only a page at a time (see Figure 5). The MORE program (MORE.COM file) must be on the current directory, or use the PATH command to find it automatically (see "Operations, PATH").

```
If you are loading other extended memory programs which do not use
the XMS interface to manage the extended memory, they should be
configured to leave at least 64K of extended memory free.

System Requirements

To use HIMEM.SYS with your computer, you need the following:

°    An IBM PC/AT, PS/2 (except models 25 and 30), or compatible
computer

°    Extended memory

Installing HIMEM.SYS

To install HIMEM.SYS, include the following command line in your
CONFIG.SYS file:

    DEVICE=[d:] [path] HIMEM.SYS [/HMAMIN=h] [/NUMHANDLES=n]

When you start your computer, the driver is loaded and the
following message is displayed:
--More--
```

Figure 5

I have a hard disk with thousands of file names in many subdirectories. I'm trying to locate a certain file name but can't remember it completely. How can I do it?

Use the system file list in DOS SHELL. Choose the system file list under Arrange. Change the Display options file name to as much of the name as you can remember with the global file characters ? and *. The ? character indicates any single character in a given position. For example, the Display option name ???? indicates any four-character file name. The * character indicates any string of characters from one to eight. For example, the Display option name ????.* indicates a four-character file name with any extension (including no extension). See Figure 6 for a typical example.

If you think the file name starts with an "A," for example, you can use the Display option A*.*, which will list all file names starting with an A. If you think that the file name starts with an A and has a .TXT extension, you could use A*.TXT. If you're certain that the file name has only two characters and starts with a D, you could use the Display option D?.*.

Be certain to do a system file display starting at the root directory, for example, selecting C:\.

```
12-01-89                    File System                    1:02 pm
 File  Options  Arrange  Exit
 Ctrl+letter selects a drive.                              F1=Help
 ⬚A  ⬚B  ▣C  ⬚D  ⬚E  ⬚F

C:\WORDPROUS\                                    A*.*         ⟦ᶻᶻ⟧
                                                             ◀◀
File                                                              ▶▶│ ➡
  Name : A.BAT      │⬚A        .BAT             23  08-06-88  8:03pm
  Attr : ....       │⬚AAAAA                  1,341  07-03-89 11:50pm
Selected          C │⬚ABSOLUTE.ASM           4,410  09-24-87  4:54pm
  Number:         0 │⬚ACKERMAN.BAS           1,026  04-02-87  1:00am
  Size :          0 │⬚AD071589.SCF           1,245  07-16-89 10:37am
Directory           │⬚AD072189.SCF           1,763  09-07-89  4:01am
  Name : US         │⬚AD072389.SCF           1,162  09-23-89  9:27am
  Size :     32,786 │⬚AD073189.SCF           1,532  07-31-89  3:27pm
  Files :        11 │⬚AD081788.SF             256  08-17-88  6:39pm
Disk                │⬚ADDCHNG                 384  04-19-89 12:32am
  Name : 040389     │⬚ADDCHNGP                384  04-19-89 12:39am
  Size : 21,309,440 │⬚ADDRESS .1            3,584  08-25-88  9:06pm
  Avail: 1,228,800  │⬚ADDRESS .1BA        11,010  08-08-88  4:52pm
  Files :     1,317 │⬚ADDRESS .1BA        11,010  08-08-88  4:52pm
  Dirs :         69 │⬚ADDRESS .BAK         3,584  08-25-88  9:06pm

 F10=Actions  Shift+F9=Command Prompt
```

Figure 6

34

I'd like to find a file containing the text "Don't lose this!," but I have 1500 files on my hard disk. Any suggestions?

It's easy to search a single file with the FIND command in command prompt mode. However, searching multiple files automatically is a more difficult problem. Here's a short batch file to search all files in the current subdirectory. Enter it with your word processor in text mode (or see "Files, Short ASCII") and call it FINDT.BAT:

```
for %%f in (*.*) do find "%%1" %%f
```

Once the file is entered, you can call it at any time from the current directory by entering the file name followed by the text sought. To search for "Don't lose this!," for example, you'd have:

```
C:\sprint>findt Don't
```

Note that only a word search can be done. All files in the current directory will be searched and any lines containing "Don't" will be listed.

Files, Full Disk

My hard disk is full. How can I make more room?

Consider these options to make more room on the drive:

- Display the files in a DOS SHELL system file list ordered by name. Delete any duplicate files.
- Examine suspicious files that may contain temporary results or garbage by the view option in the DOS SHELL (use a special file name, such as SCRATCH, for ease of deletion in the future). The date of creation may be a clue to its contents.
- Delete files that are present in applications, but never used. For example, a word processor subdirectory may contain 24 printer drivers but only one may be necessary for your system printer. Delete any READ.ME or documentation files that repeat information found in manuals.
- Move seldom used applications or data to floppy disk archival storage and delete the programs from the drive.
- Combine many short text files into a single large file by using the COPY command in command prompt mode:

```
C:\>copy accts.jan+accts.feb accts89
   (combines two files in one).
```

I go through my disk periodically and try to weed out duplicated files. How can I tell if files are equivalent?

A fairly good way to do this is to compare the creation date, time, and size of two files, even if they have different names. If the creation date, creation time, and size are the same in the two files, then the files are the same. The only cases in which this would not be true is if one file was modified and written instantly after the original file, but the two files would have to be written within a minute of each other. Even if the date and time are incorrect, the clock is running and will tag a file with a current time.

The time of file creation is not displayed in DOS SHELL file displays, so the command prompt DIR command must be used to see the creation time.

Although it's overkill in some cases, the COMP command in command prompt mode will compare one file with another on a byte by byte basis and tell you if the files compare or if they are different. A typical example is:

```
C:\>comp let08239.txt letter1.txt
```

Are there any naming conventions for files? I have 500 files on my hard disk, and I'm starting to get confused about what I have and where to find it.

There are no naming conventions for the main part of the file name. However, there are conventions for the file name extension (the three characters after the period). .SYS files are system files, .EXE and .COM files are executable files, .BAT files are batch files, .OBJ files are object files, .LIB files are library files, and .LNK files are linker files. In addition, these extensions are often used: .BAK for backup files, .DOC for documentation files, and .ME for READ.ME files. Also, there may be conventions for extensions within an application program. Other than dedicated system extensions, any one to three letters may be used. It may be convenient to establish your own usage conventions for file name extensions.

Short file names are easy to enter but there are several disadvantages. For example, there are fewer combinations, only a thousand or so for two letter file names such as PS.TXT. Many users favor eight characters for the main file name plus three characters for the extension. There can be a lot of information relating to the use of the file in eleven characters, as in SCRNDUMP.001, SCRNDUMP.002, INCTAX 89.JAN, and PAYABLES.MAR.

Don't forget that the same file name may be used in different directories (see "Files, Subdirectory Format").

Is there a way to protect my files so they cannot be deleted or modified? I have some critical data that I want to save.

Yes, there is. Each file has a read-only status associated with it. You can mark the file "read only" so that the file can be read but not deleted or modified.

To change the read-only status from the DOS SHELL, select one or more files from the File display and then choose the Change Attribute item from the File menu. Select option 2 to change all files. Highlight Read-Only from the Hidden, Read-Only, Archive menu by the arrow keys and press the space bar to mark the file Read-Only (you'll see a small triangle to the left of the Read Only text). See Figure 3. Now press <ENTER> to make the change. DOS will change all files selected to read-only files. After these changes, users of the system will be able to view the files or a program may read from them, but they cannot be deleted or modified.

You can easily change the read-only attributes back to read and write by performing the Change Attribute procedure again, this time resetting the read-only attribute.

I have about 100 files that must be renamed from the form ACCT001.BIL to the form SAVE001.BAK. Is there any easy way to do this other than using the DOS SHELL to rename 100 individual files?

Yes, there is an easy and extremely rapid way by using the command prompt mode. Use the two "wild card" characters * and ? and the DOS RENAME command. The ? character denotes a single character in a file name. The * character denotes from one to eight characters. Your new file names differ in the first four characters and the extension. The command:

```
C:\>rename acct???.bil save???.bak
```

will search for all seven-character file names that start with "ACCT" and have the extension ".BIL." When a file name is found, it will be renamed with "SAVE", the fourth through seventh characters of the original file name, and the new extension ".BAK." File name ACCT001.BIL, for example, will be renamed SAVE001.BAK.

This procedure works for any renaming where there's a group of files with similar names. This command, for example, renames all files starting with an "A" to files starting with a "B," keeping the same extension

```
C:\>rename a*.* b*.*
```

While using the system I created a lot of files with the wrong date and time entered. Is there any way of correcting the date and time in the files?

Every time a file is updated, the current time and date are recorded in the disk directory for that file. This date and time is carried along throughout all subsequent copies of that file.

You can start over by reading in and modifying each file. It's not sufficient to simply read in the file, however. The file must be modified, however slightly. You can add a space and then delete it in a word processing file, for example. The application program senses any modifications and makes the proper DOS communication. The corresponding directory entry then will have the current date and time. This method doesn't work for files that cannot be modified.

Another way is somewhat involved, but works. Change the date and time to any previous (or future) date. Now use the command prompt COPY command as follows:

```
C:\>copy thisfile.txt + nul
```

This command recopies the file by adding a NUL file (essentially nothing) to it, but fools the system into thinking the file has been changed! The file directory entry will be changed to the current date and time. Reset the time and date after the procedure.

How can I create a short AUTOEXEC.BAT, CONFIG.SYS, or batch file without having to go through my word processor?

You can go directly from keyboard to a disk file for very short files by using the COPY command in command prompt mode. Suppose you want to create a batch file to change the default directory to C:\TURBOC and then execute a program called TC.EXE. You'd enter:

```
C:\>copy con: clang.bat<ENTER>
cd c:\turboc<ENTER>
tc<ENTER>
^Z
```

The COPY CON: CLANG tells DOS to accept line input from the keyboard, each line being terminated with an <ENTER> character. The output goes to disk file CLANG.BAT, a batch file. The next two lines are batch file lines that change the directory and execute TC.EXE. Pressing the Ctrl key followed by the Z key terminates the input. You now have created the two-line file CLANG.BAT. The same approach works for any file. However, with this method there is limited editing on a line basis only. You can backspace (left arrow), space right (right arrow), insert (Ins), and delete (Del).

Do you have any suggestions for the arrangement of files on a hard disk?

Many users agree that the *root* directory of the hard disk should contain mostly subdirectories, except for commonly used resident programs such as Sidekick, the CONFIG.SYS file, and .BAT files. There are several good reasons for this: it's hard to wade through dozens of files to find the right one, even with the capabilities of the shell. Also, many files can be logically grouped. For example, you'd want all word processing files together and not mixed with program files. Another good reason for having a tree structure is that files in different subdirectories can have the same name. You might have two files calledC:\ROOT\ACCOUNTS \TELLIST.TEL and C:\ROOT\PERSONAL \TELLIST.TEL;the file name of each is TELLIST.TEL, which would not be possible with one huge directory. Also remember that the root directory can have only 112 separate files or subdirectories before it runs out of room; subdirectories can have an unlimited number of entries.

Many users also agree that it's probably not good to have *too* many levels of subdirectories. It's just as inefficient to have a directory called "C:\ROOT\BILL\PERSONAL\CAR\REPAIRS\ 1988\AUGUST\HYUNDAI\MOTOR" and to find a single file therein, as it is to have that file mixed with hundreds.

How can I convert the hexadecimal view of a file to something meaningful?

The hexadecimal display in the DOS SHELL view function (use the F9 key to switch between hexadecimal and ASCII) shows the displacement of bytes in a file on the left, the contents of the file in hexadecimal in the middle, and the ASCII text of the file on the right. See Figure 7 for a typical display.

Each two hexadecimal digits represents one byte of data. For text files, a single character is held in one byte. Each hexadecimal digit may be 0, 1, 2, 3, 4, 5, 6, 7, 8, 9, A, B, C, D, E, or F (0 through 15). To find the equivalent decimal value, multiply the first digit by 16 and add the second digit.

Displayable text characters are hexadecimal codes 20 through 7F and represent special characters (spaces, asterisk, pound sign, etc.), the digits 0 through 9, upper-case characters, and lower-case characters. Check the hexadecimal value with the corresponding location on the right. Non-displayable characters are represented on the right by a period.

Text files also include the 0D character (carriage return) and 0A character (line feed). These normally terminate a line.

Bytes in non-text files can represent virtually any type of special coding including machine-language instructions and system codes.

```
                      File View

   To view a file's content press [Enter] or [Space].

   Viewing file: C:\CONFIG.SYS


000000  42524541 4B3D4F4E 0D0A4255 46464552  BREAK.ON..BUFFER
000010  533D3230 0D0A4649 4C45533D 380D0A4C  S.20..FILES.8..L
000020  41535444 52495645 3D460D0A 5348454C  ASTDRIVE.F..SHEL
000030  4C3D433A 5C444F53 5C434F4D 4D414E44  L.C..DOS.COMMAND
000040  2E434F4D 202F5020 2F453A32 35360D0A  .COM.P..E.256..
000050  44455649 43453D43 3A5C444F 535C414D  DEVICE.C..DOS.AM
000060  53492E53 59530D0A 494E5354 414C4C3D  SI.SYS..INSTALL.
000070  433A5C44 4F535C46 4153544F 50454E2E  C..DOS.FASTOPEN.
000080  45584520 433A3D35 302C3235 0D0A0D0A  EXE.C..50.25...
000090  44455649 43453D44 52495645 522E5359  DEVICE.DRIVER.SY
0000A0  53202F44 3A310D0A 44455649 43453D43  S..D.1.DEVICE.C
0000B0  3A5C474D 4F555345 2E535953 0D0A4445  ..GMOUSE.SYS..DE
0000C0  56494345 3D433A5C 444F535C 56444953  VICE.C..DOS.VDIS

<┘=Enter  Esc=Cancel  F9=Hex/ASCII
```

Figure 7

46

Chapter 4

Floppy Disks

Floppy Disks, Adding

I have an IBM PC-XT compatible with two 5.25 inch floppy disk drives. I'd like to replace one of the floppy drives with a 3.5 inch drive. Will DOS support this?

Yes, DOS *will* support a 3.5 inch drive in either 720K byte or 1.44M byte format. However, older floppy disk drive controllers may only support the 720K byte format. A 720K byte 3.5 inch drive can usually be added directly in place of the 5.25 inch drive from a hardware standpoint; the cable connections are usually the same. Verify this compatibility before purchase.

Once you have added the drive, it's necessary to add two special lines in the CONFIG.SYS file (see "Startup, Modifying CONFIG.SYS Files") for the new second physical diskette drive:

```
LASTDRIVE=D
DEVICE=DRIVER.SYS /D:1
```

Once this line is added, a special driver will be loaded on system start and the drive will be assigned drive specifier D:. (You should see the message "Loaded external disk driver for drive D" on startup.) Use this drive specifier for all operations to the drive.

I'm confused about how much data I can actually get on a floppy disk. Can all the 360K bytes or 720K bytes be used?

A "K" is not 1000 but 1024. A 360K byte disk is therefore 360 x 1024 = 368,640 bytes and not 360,000 - about 2.5 percent more.

If you have a 360K byte disk without system files to begin with, you can use all of the 368,640 bytes less that used for disk directories and a table called the File Allocation Table. This amounts to about 362,496 bytes.

If you have a 720K byte disk without system files the available space for data is 730,112 bytes of the 737,280 bytes available.

If the /S option is used in formatting the diskette, three system files are added: two hidden files that don't show up on the directory and COMMAND.COM. These files take up about 110,000 bytes.

However, space is allocated on the disk in 1024 byte chunks. Since all files are not even multiples of 1024 bytes, about 512 bytes is wasted (on the average) for every disk file used.

To sum it all up, figure upon using about 337,000 bytes for a 360K diskette, 680,000 bytes for a 720K diskette, 1,140,000 bytes for a 1.2M diskette, and 1,377,824 bytes for a 1.44M diskette if system files are not on the disk. Subtract about 110,000 bytes from this figure if system files are to be included.

Floppy Disks, Fragmentation

I have a database on a floppy diskette that involves a lot of processing. It seems the more I work with it, the slower the access becomes.

You may have a problem with *fragmentation* of data or program files. On a new disk, DOS allocates segments of the disk that are contiguous - located next to each other physically. This means that disk head movement, a time consuming process relative to computer speed, is minimized. However, as data is deleted and new data added, DOS allocates disk space wherever available. The result is a chain of data segments spread over available space on the entire disk. Accessing this data involves a lot of disk head movement.

A DISKCOPY simply duplicates a diskette. And any fragmentation. You can eliminate fragmentation by starting with a clean, newly formatted diskette and then doing a copy of all files on the disk by a series of COPYs or XCOPYs. Each data or program file will be allocated a contiguous block of disk space without fragmentation. This procedure can be done periodically but does not have to be done for each disk backup.

When doing a copy by this method, use a FORMAT /S if the new disk is to contain system files (if it is to be a "bootable" diskette).

I keep getting "Invalid media or track 0 bad" when I attempt to FORMAT the same diskette. What should I do?

Throw it away. Diskettes are inexpensive enough so that you should not take chances with saving your important data. Besides that, DOS FORMAT simply will not begin to format a diskette on which it cannot put the directory and FAT (File Allocation Table). These elements are mandatory on any disk.

DOS FORMAT is more tolerant for other disk errors, making an entry in the FAT that prevents defective sectors from being allocated as portions of files. You *could*, therefore, use diskettes that have bad sectors, although the total disk space would be reduced slightly. However, many experienced users believe that if you have any bad sectors during a diskette FORMAT, the diskette is suspect and should be thrown away.

Floppy Disks, Not Ready Reading Drive

I keep getting a "Not ready reading drive A:" error when attempting to read a diskette. What am I doing wrong?

We hate to mention an obvious thing such as this, but it's happened to us. Make certain that the disk door is shut on a 5.25 inch drive and that the diskette is inserted all the way into the drive for a 3.5 inch drive.

Another problem that could cause the error is if the disk is inserted upside down in the drive. There is a right way and a wrong way for diskettes. On a 5.25 inch diskette, the write protect notch should be on the left while on a 3.5 inch diskette the write protect switch also should be on the left, for horizontally mounted drives.

An infrequent condition that might cause the problem is slight misalignment of the write protect notch on a 5.25 inch diskette. Try another diskette as a check.

I have a friend with a PS/2 system with a 1.44M byte 3.5 inch drive. My system has a 720K byte 3.5 inch drive. Is there any way to read his 1.44M byte diskettes?

No, not on your drive. The disk and disk controller for a 720K byte drive simply will not handle the higher density of the 1.44M diskettes. Have your friend copy his diskettes on twice the number of 720K byte diskettes. He can use the less expensive 720K byte double density diskettes to do so instead of the high density diskettes. The procedure for this is given in "Utilities, Copying a 720K byte Diskette in a 1.44M Drive."

The resulting diskettes should be fully usable *for reading* in your system. However, if he used the /S option in the FORMAT, you may have a problem. Although the disks created can be read in your system, they may not be "bootable" unless you both have IBM systems. PC-DOS 4.X will not necessarily run on non-IBM systems and vice versa.

You may have to recopy the diskettes, using command prompt COPY *.*, after formatting your own diskettes with the /S option.

Floppy Disks, Reading Incompatible 5.25 inch Diskettes

I have friend with an AT type system with a 1.2M byte 5.25 inch drive. My system has a 360K byte 5.25 inch drive. Is there any way to read his 1.2M byte diskettes?

No, not on your drive. Have him copy the 1.2M diskettes onto three times the number of 360K byte double-sided, double-density diskettes. He should use the /1 option in command prompt FORMAT to format the diskettes and then use COPY *.* to copy the files. He should not use the /S option, unless you both have IBM systems. However, here's the catch: The diskettes produced may not be read reliably in a 5.25 inch 360K byte drive! Try reading the diskettes and if you can, recopy the data on them onto your own diskettes after formatting them. Use the command prompt COPY *.* command. Then throw the original diskettes in the trash compactor.

On some diskettes I get occasional seek errors. What's happening?

A seek error is a serious disk error. It means that the disk driver attempted to find a particular physical track by a seek operation (moving the head) and could not find the proper track.

Seek errors for floppy disks sometimes occur when a floppy disk is copied on one system and run on another. If the seek error occurred with a commercial software program, it may mean that your floppy disk needs alignment or technical adjustment. Any moderate to large-sized software company usually produces diskettes from properly calibrated equipment. If the seek error occurred with disks from another system, either the source or destination (your) drive may need adjustment. If the seek error occurred with your own disks and the disks were produced months or years ago, your disk drive may have gone out of adjustment over that period.

This type of problem is no longer as bad as it once was. Modern floppy disk drives are mechanically better than their ancestors ten years ago, but this problem still occasionally occurs.

What volume label should be used when doing a format to a floppy disk?

Unlike volume labels on hard disks, which serve little purpose (the hard disk is there but it's not removable), volume labels on diskettes *are* useful. Up to 11 characters can be used as a diskette volume label, so you can give the diskette a useful name such as UTILITIES, SEPTEMBER89, or WORDPRO1. The volume label is always displayed as upper case.

The volume label of any disk can be read at any time by theVOL command, as a check to see that the proper diskette is being used:

```
C:\>vol a:
```

I'm trying to save a file on diskette but I get a write protect error? What does this mean?

It's a long tradition in computers to provide a physical means to protect a magnetic tape or diskette from being written over. It's akin to write protecting your copy of Star Wars on video cassette tape. On 5.25 inch diskette there's a *write-protect notch on one side*. This notch is covered with a tab of sticky material to keep the diskette from being overwritten. (Use an Avery label if you can't find a tab.) If the tab is not present, the diskette can be formatted, used to make a copy of another diskette, or used as a destination to save files. On commercial software, the write protect notch often is not even present to ensure that the diskette can never be written to.

A 3.5 inch diskette has another arrangement for write protection. There's a small switch which can be pushed back and forth by a fingernail or pencil point. When the switch is at the furthest position away from the end that is inserted into the drive, the diskette is write protected. In the opposite position, the diskette can be formatted, used for a copy of another diskette, or used as a destination to save files.

Chapter 5

Hard Disks

Hard Disks,Errors

I am getting disk errors when attempting to read my hard disk and I have not done a recent backup. Nothing seems to help. How can I retrieve my data?

First of all, don't do anything more. Actions such as executing a CHKDSK /F command may make the problem worse. Start with this realization: You may have lost all of the data on your disk.

If the data on disk is crucial, consider employing a computer consulting service to retrieve the data. There are companies that will attempt to retrieve files from hard disk. In this case, leave the disk as is and do not attempt to access it further.

If the data are important, but not crucial, obtain a copy of the Norton Utilities from most software dealers. This set of repair programs may allow you to recover some or all of your data. Complete instructions are included.

If only a few files appear to be bad, stop where you are and backup the remaining files with a good general-purpose backup utility, such as Fifth Generation System's Fastback. Fastback will continue even if a number of files are bad, unlike the BACKUP command in DOS. After backup, reformat the hard disk; if disk errors are encountered during this reformat, you may have to do a *low-level format* . Low-level formatting is described in documentation included with the disk drive and has appeared in personal computer publications such as *PC Magazine*. The procedure is dependent upon your system hardware and is therefore too extensive to be described here.

How can I find out which files are fragmented on my hard disk?

Fragmented files are those disk files that do not exist as one contiguous block of disk space (see "Hard Disks, Fragmentation"). To find out whether your files are fragmented, use the command prompt command CHKDSK with this format:

```
C:\>chkdsk *.*
```

The above command will check only those files in the *current directory*. If you are in a subdirectory called C:\SPRINT, for example, only files in that directory will be checked. If any fragmented files are found, DOS will report the file name and amount of fragmentation:

```
C:\SPRINT\OP.OVL Contains 8
      noncontiguous blocks
```

Follow the procedures in "Hard Disks, Fragmentation" to "de-frag" your files. Another option is to use the procedures in such programs as Norton Utilities, PC-Tools, or Mace.

I used CHKDSK in command prompt mode to fix my hard disk recently, and it fixed it all right - I wound up with an unusable disk!

CHKDSK can be used to analyze the contents of your hard disk (or diskettes). If CHKDSK is used without the /F option, it simply reports on the contents of the disk and any errors found in the disk directory and file allocation table. CHKDSK is an inherently good program!

If CHKDSK is used with the /F (fix) option, however, as in,

```
C:\>chkdsk /f
```

it will not only find errors, but attempt to fix them. If you have a disk controller or disk drive that is going bad, this cure may be worse than the disease. A recommended procedure is to use CHKDSK without the /F option first to see if any errors are found. If errors are found, take the time to do a disk backup before proceeding. *Then* run CHKDSK with the /F option, or use one of the commercially available disk correction programs that take fixes a step at a time and are more polite in asking you how to proceed.

I have a database on a hard disk that involves a lot of processing. It seems the more I work with it, the slower the access becomes.

This is the identical fragmentation problem as on a floppy disk, but on a larger scale. On a newly formatted hard disk, DOS allocates segments of the disk that are contiguous - located next to each other physically. Disk head movement, a time consuming process relative to computer speed, is minimized. As data is deleted and new data added, however, DOS allocates disk space wherever available. The result is a chain of data segments spread over available space on the entire hard disk. Accessing this data involves a lot of disk head movement and a great deal of time.

Eliminate fragmentation by starting with a clean, newly formatted hard disk and then transferring all files to the hard disk from scratch. Each data or program file will be allocated a contiguous block of disk space without fragmentation. After a backup by SAVE or another backup application program (such as Fastback), reformat the hard disk. Don't forget to include the /S option if the disk is the primary hard disk. Now do the restore operation. Warning: Do not do the reformatting if the backup is an *incremental* backup that saves only selected files.

Hard Disks, How Often Should They Be Reformatted?

My hard disk has been giving me occasional errors. I've made backups, but I'm afraid of the situation getting worse. Am I justified?

While there are differences of opinion regarding the reliability of hard disks, here are some tips for maintaining data on your hard disk:

• Nothing lasts forever, even hard disk data. You will lose some or all of your hard disk data eventually. There are two general types of hard disks: MFM format (10M bytes, 20M bytes, etc.) and RLL format (30M bytes, etc.). Typical MFM drives last for a year or two without problems, while typical RLL drives last for six months to a year.

• Listen to your hard disk. If errors are occurring more frequently, the disk may be on its way to a major failure.

• Errors often occur if a hard disk is moved physically. Moving your computer from a horizontal to vertical (tower) position may result in hard disk errors. You'll need to start from low-level formatting (see "Hard Disks, Types of Formatting") through FDISK and FORMAT if you change the position this radically.

• Leaving your hard disk on permanently appears to result in fewer pieces of minute debris being "kicked up" to cause disk failures.

• ALWAYS BACKUP YOUR HARD DISK ON A PERIODIC BASIS (see "Utilities, Backup").

I cannot FORMAT my hard disk. I keep getting the message "Invalid media or track 0 bad". What should I do?

This is a serious problem. First, read "Hard Disks, How Often Should They Be Reformatted"?. If you recently moved your hard disk or cabinet, put it back in the same position and try FORMAT again. If there is an extreme in temperature in your room, try a FORMAT at a more normal temperature. Check disk cables; you may want to reseat them if you're a handy hardware type. About the only action to take from this point is to try a low-level format, FDISK, and then FORMAT again.

I run CHKDSK periodically to "clean up" my disk. The last time I ran it, DOS reported lost allocation units and asked if I wanted to recover the lost data. I replied yes, but I'm not sure what I have or what to do with it.

CHKDSK checks disk file allocation, bad sectors, and generally reports on the number of disk files and disk space. Lost allocation units can be created by programs that do not handle files properly. For example, a program may ask DOS to allocate space for a file, but then never complete the operation (*close* the file). DOS returns the lost allocation units to the pool of available disk space and creates new files labeled FILE0000.CHK, FILE0001.CHK, and so forth.

You should View these files from the DOS SHELL in both ASCII and hexadecimal mode (use the F9 key to switch) to see what they represent. You may be able to salvage text files by reading them into your word processor and doing some editing and linking. There's a good chance, however, that the lost clusters are simply garbage. If the files appear to be portions of good files, you may have software problems in applications programs.

I want to add a hard disk to my system, but I'm a little concerned about adding one that's too big. What's the maximum size that will run under DOS?

Prior to DOS 4.0, the maximum hard disk size that DOS would accommodate was 32M bytes (33,554,432 bytes). Disk space above that size could not be accessed by DOS. However, DOS 4.0 allows support for hard disk sizes up to 2,199,023,256,000 bytes (2,097,152M bytes)!

The only practical limiting factor for DOS 4.0 hard disks is therefore cost and availability. Common hard disk sizes of 40M, 80M, and 120M bytes are not a problem in DOS 4.0. One advisory note: If you have DOS 4.00, be certain to upgrade to DOS 4.01 (see "Startup, DOS 4.0 Corrections") to correct possible errors in creating partitions of exactly 32M bytes.

Hard Disks, Not Ready Reading Drive

I get a "Not ready reading drive C:" error when attempting to read my hard disk! Is my disk destroyed?

No, there's hope. This usually indicates a cabling, drive electronics, or controller electronics problem. The data is probably on disk, but the system doesn't get back the proper ready signal from the drive. You may have to get expert hardware help on this one. However, if you are at all mechanically and electrically inclined, open the cabinet to access the disk. Remove any mounting screws and slide the drive forward enough to get access to the two data cables connected to the drive. Carefully pull these off (noting the orientation) and clean the pc board edge connectors with a large eraser. Reseat the connectors and try again. If this doesn't help, you may have a bad electronics board in the drive, or a bad controller board, both of which will require some expert help. Let the repair service know that you want to save the data on disk if this is the case!

I have an 80M byte hard disk. I ran FDISK and "partitioned" all of the disk for DOS. Just what is a partition and why would I want more than one?

A partition is simply a way to divide the disk up into different areas. One of the main reasons you might want to make more than one partition is to run another operating system. For example, it's possible to run an operating system called Xenix on IBM PC compatibles as well as DOS, and there are special-purpose operating systems as well. In most cases, however, users will want to run just DOS and the entire disk can be devoted to a single DOS partition. FDISK makes it easy for you to do this by assuming that you'll want to devote the entire diskette to DOS.

I keep getting "Seek errors" on my hard disk. How do I correct them?

A seek error is a serious disk error. It means that the disk driver attempted to find a particular physical track by a seek operation (moving the head) and could not find the proper track. It may mean that the disk needs to be reformatted by a FORMAToperation or by a low-level format (see "Hard Disks, How Often Should They Be Reformatted?").

If you physically moved the disk, move it back to the same position and orientation. If the ambient temperature has radically changed, try the operation at a temperature approaching normal conditions. If the seek errors do not occur at all times, you may want to find conditions during which the disk operates without seek errors and then make a quick BACKUP (see "Utilities, Backup"). Once you've captured the contents of the disk, you can proceed to define the problem without losing data (see "Hard Disks, Fixing with CHKDSK").

I have a single floppy, single hard disk system. My hard disk just crashed and I cannot boot the system. Where do I go from here?

First, read "Hard Disks, Errors" to see if you can salvage any data if you've not made a recent backup. FORMATTING WILL COMPLETELY DESTROY ANY PROGRAMS OR DATA YOU HAVE ON DISK!

You'll need a copy of DOS on floppy to start. Follow the procedure given in "Getting Started with DOS" to create DOS on diskettes. You will not need to run the SHELL and will primarily be concerned with the Startup diskette and the FDISK and FORMAT commands. You'll have one or two diskettes containing DOS.

Next, you'll need to boot DOS from diskette. Put the Startup diskette in drive A: and boot by pressing the Ctrl, Alt, and Del keys.

Now run FDISK by entering:

```
A:\>fdisk
```

All programs are on a 1.44M byte diskette, if this is your drive, two 720K byte diskettes, or four 360K byte diskettes. If FDISK is not found, it is one of the other diskettes. Do an:

```
A:\>dir
```

to find the right diskette. Now re-enter the command. Once FDISK is running, follow the

71

menu choices to create a DOS partition with the maximum size. If disk errors occur in FDISK, see "Hard Disks, How Often Should They be Reformatted?" Exit FDISK by pressing the Esc key.

Now run the FORMAT program by:

```
A:\>format /s
```

If FORMAT is not found, it is one of the other diskettes. Find FORMAT.COM by a DIR and put the proper diskette in drive A:. Re-enter the command. When asked if you really want to proceed with format, press Y followed by <ENTER>. See "Hard Disks, Volume Label" for information on the volume label. If major disk errors occur during formatting, see the reference given above.

Turn system power off, wait 10 seconds, and turn power on. The system should reboot with the DOS title message (but not DOS SHELL) and then display:

```
C:\>
```

If formatting is successful, you now can Install DOS 4.0 to hard disk by following the procedures in "Getting Started With DOS 4.0." After you've installed DOS on hard disk, you can RESTORE your files or rebuild the disk contents from scratch.

I see references to a "low-level" formatting of hard disk. Is that the same as what is done in the Format utility?

No, it is not. A hard disk drive initially is a disk of magnetic material without any pattern. There are no sectors or tracks that exist on the disk physically.

When the computer manufacturer or disk drive/controller manufacturer buys disk drives, he must do a low-level formatting to establish the tracks and sectors on the disk, along with other data to help in the read/write process. You can look upon this as a way of establishing skeleton tracks and sectors on the disk.

The FDISK program *partitions* the disk space into one or more areas dedicated to DOS and possibly other operating systems.

The FORMAT program now completes the process by testing tracks, adding a directory and file allocation table, and adding three system files if the /S option is used.

Often just doing an FDISK and FORMAT will restore a hard disk after errors or a disk "crash," but the disk may have physical alignment problems that require a low-level reformat - a type of calibration.

The low-level format can be done by following a step-by-step procedure using DEBUG which is usually found in disk controller documentation. Your computer dealer also should be able to help.

What volume label should be used when doing a format to a hard disk?

The volume label was used originally to label magnetic tapes and removable disk packs on large mainframe computers. The concept has carried over into the small computer area, even though it is less practical here, where most "mass storage" media is a single hard disk, not removable. For that reason, don't be too concerned about the volume label for a hard disk - it's not going anywhere! A practical label to provide is the date of formatting, such as 06-17-1989. Up to 11 characters can be used.

You can read the volume label (and creation date, if used) by the command prompt command:

```
C:\>vol c:
```

Chapter 6

Mouse

Mouse, Cursor, But Doesn't Move

I want to use a mouse in DOS SHELL. The system loads fine, but the cursor for the mouse remains at the upper left-hand corner of the screen.

Check your DOSSHELL.BAT file, usually located in C:\DOS. It should contain a mouse driver option similar to the "MOS" text in the following:

```
@SHELLC /MOS:PCMSDRV.MOS/CO3/COLOR/
    TRAN/DOS/MENU/MUL/SND/
    MEU:SHELL.MEU/CLR:SHELL.CLR/
    PROMPT/MAINT/EXIT/SWAP/DATE
```

The mouse driver name should be the proper one for the type of mouse you are using (see "Mouse, Installation in DOS").

If there is a mouse driver and you do get a cursor (an arrow in EGA or VGA screen mode or a shaded area in CGA text mode) it means that DOS has successfully loaded the Mouse Driver and recognized the fact that you want mouse operation. It has even drawn the cursor on the screen. The problem is, therefore, in the hardware. Check your mouse cabling to make certain there are no breaks and that it plugs in firmly to the serial port connector or controller board connector. If the cabling seems all right, you may have a problem in the mouse itself or mouse controller (bus mouse).

When double-clicking my mouse, it takes several tries to select a menu item. Single-click selection seems to be no problem.

This problem seems to occur when the mouse is clicked and then moves slightly after the first click and before the second click. Evidently DOS compares the position of each click and acts on the double click only if the two positions are the same. To solve the problem, press harder on the mouse while double clicking so that the mouse does not move.

Another solution is to reduce the resolution of your mouse to a lower value. Most mice have variable resolutions of 200 to 1200 dots per inch. Refer to your mouse reference manual for instructions on how to reset the resolution; usually this involves adding a parameter value while initializing the mouse driver in the AUTOEXEC.BAT file (see "Startup, Modifying AUTOEXEC.BAT ").

Mouse, How to Use

I just installed a mouse on my system, but I'm having some trouble figuring out how to use it with the DOS SHELL displays.

Some people are mystified by mice, but they're mainly "point and click." First of all, a mouse isn't tied in to table or mouse pad locations at all. If you run off the edge of the table, just pick up the mouse and place it back on the table in any location!

Use the mouse to position the mouse cursor (an arrow in EGA or VGA displays or a shaded area in CGA text displays) over the choice on the screen. In the DOS SHELL, a choice is indicated by a list of selections, a selection box, or a selection with no box around it (F10=Actions). Clicking the left-hand button on the mouse will highlight one of the items in a list or select an action from a box or other type of selection. Rapidly clicking the left-hand button twice will select the item in a list (such as File System from the main display). The two-click operation must be about as fast as you can say "one-one."

Sometimes a mouse will slide after the first click and reposition itself to the next item. In this case, it will appear as if you have not double-clicked on an item in a list. Press harder on the mouse to prevent it from moving and try again.

How Do I Install a Mouse Software Driver in DOS?

A software driver program is necessary for mouse operation. After installing the mouse hardware (see "Mouse, Which One?"), follow the manufacturer's directions for adding a software driver, which should be supplied on disk with the mouse. Usually this simply involves entering a single command such as,

```
C:\>gmouse
```

to initialize the driver. This command also should be entered in the AUTOEXEC.BAT file (see "Startup, Modifying AUTOEXEC.BAT "). The mouse now will work with non-DOS programs that support a mouse. To install with DOS, continue reading here.

DOS contains three built-in drivers in files PCIBMDRV. MOS (PC mouse), PCMSDRV. MOS (Microsoft serial mouse), and PCMSPDRV. MOS (Microsoft parallel (bus) mouse). Include the startup options /MOS:PCMSDRV. MOS or /MOS:PCMSDRV. MOS or /MOS:PCMSPDRV. MOS in the DOSSHELL.BAT file. Each of these loads in the proper mouse driver. A typical startup line containing such a mouse driver option is:

```
@SHELLC /MOS:PCMSDRV.MOS/CO3/TRAN/
DOS/MENU/MUL/SND/MEU:SHELL.MEU
/CLR:SHELL.CLR/PROMPT/MAINT/EXIT/
SWAP/DATE
```

If you are adding a mouse to the second serial port, also add the option /COM2 to the startup line.

After rebooting the system, you should see an arrow (graphics mode) or shaded area (text mode) indicating the mouse is active. See Figure 8. Move the mouse and you should see the mouse pointer move on the screen.

```
 12-01-89              Start Programs              1:01 pm
 Program  Group  Exit                              F1=Help
                         Main Group
           To select an item, use the up and down arrows.
        To start a program or display a new group, press Enter.

 Command Prompt
 File System
 Change Colors
 DOS Utilities...          ⌖




 F10=Actions          Shift+F9=Command Prompt
```

Figure 8

I want to add a mouse to my system. Which one can I use with DOS?

DOS can handle three types of mice: an IBM mouse, a Microsoft serial mouse, or a Microsoft parallel mouse. Most manufacturers, such as Genius, Mouse Systems, or Logitech, make mice that are compatible with the Microsoft mouse, Make certain that the mouse you purchase is a PC or Microsoft-compatible mouse that will work in an IBM PC-compatible system. If your system has two serial ports, a serial mouse can be connected to the second (COM2) port. If your system has one serial port, you'll have to disconnect any existing serial device (such as a modem) and plug in the mouse every time you want to use it, or you'll have to buy a serial switch box. A parallel mouse is connected to the system with a bus interface card that takes up a card slot. All mice come with software drivers designed for the mouse and compatible with the PC or Microsoft mouse.

Install the mouse hardware by following the manufacturer's directions. Usually this involves connecting a single cable from the serial mouse to a serial port or plugging in the bus card and cable for the parallel (bus) mouse.

See "Mouse, Installation in DOS" for directions on using a mouse with DOS.

Mouse, Why No Cursor?

I recently installed a mouse in my DOS system. However, there's no pointer on the DOS SHELL screens, just a shaded area that moves.

The mouse cursor is a pointer on EGA and VGA graphics screens, but a shaded area on text screens (▓). There is no way to create a pointer on text screens since graphics cannot be drawn and there is no pointer in the character set. DOS uses a standard character (shaded area) to represent the location of the mouse. If you move the mouse, you'll notice that the current cursor position jumps from character position to character position.

If you have EGA or VGA graphics in your system and still have the text screen, refer to "Displays, EGA Not Present" or "Displays, VGA Not Present."

Chapter 7

Operations

Operations, Access Denied Error

I share a system with several other people. We have a master file on hard disk which is updated by all users. The application program can read the file, but then replies with the error message "Access denied" when I try to update it with new data. What's happening?

The file has been protected by making it a read-only file. It cannot be deleted or updated. Perhaps a user attempted to ensure that the file would not be deleted, and in doing so, prevented it from being updated as well. See "Files, Protecting" for information on how to reset the read-only attribute of the file.

This message also appears when user or program attempts to execute a subdirectory in place of a file. Subdirectories are indicated by less than and greater than signs (<>) in both the DOS SHELL and command prompt DIR displays.

How can I automatically start my word processor whenever I power up or restart my system?

Whenever an MS-DOS system is started on power up or by pressing the Ctrl, Alt, and Del keys, it goes through a sequence of reading the CONFIG.SYS file to set system parameters and the AUTOEXEC.BAT file to load and run device drivers and other necessary programs. These actions are "built-in" the haredware system.

If you used the INSTALL program to create DOS, you probably also created an AUTOEXEC.BAT file that contained a line to load the DOS SHELL. The last three lines of a typical AUTOEXEC.BAT are:

```
PRINT /D:LPT1
GMOUSE
DOSSHELL
```

The last line starts the DOS SHELL by running the DOSSHELL.BAT batch file. Delete this line and add the appropriate lines for your word processor. For example, add one to change to the subdirectory containing the word processor and another to start execution:

```
. . .
PRINT /D:LPT1
GMOUSE
CD C:\WORDPERF
WP
```

The system will now "boot up" with your word processor. The DOS SHELL can be started at any time by:

```
C:\>c:\dosshell
```

I'm just starting to come out of my (DOS) SHELL and am trying to enter commands in command prompt mode. However, I keep getting the error message "Bad command or file name error". What's wrong?

The command prompt mode requires spaces between the actual command and other parameters. For example:

```
C:\>dira:
```

is not valid. DOS will assume that a file is to be executed called DIRA:. It will look for that file, and will respond with the error message when it is not found. Use a space between parameters and the command when in doubt:

```
C:\>dir a:
```

It's almost always correct to use lower-case (small letters), by the way.

I have several hundred files I want to copy to a diskette. However, when attempting to do this, I get the error message "Cannot make directory entry." Why?

There are two types of directories: the root directory and subdirectories. The root directory is the highest level directory; it contains files and possibly subdirectories. These subdirectories may contain other files and other subdirectories. For the most part, the root directory looks much the same as a subdirectory. The root directory, however, can hold only 112 file names, unlike a subdirectory, which can contain an unlimited number.

You need to create one or more subdirectories in the root directory of your diskette. This can be done through the create directory function in the DOS SHELL or by the MD (Make Directory) function in command prompt mode. You now can add all of the files to one or more subdirectories.

Most users believe that the root directory should contain as few files as possible and primarily hold subdirectories. It makes for a more orderly grouping of data.

I used a password for creating a Group of programs in DOS SHELL and now I can't remember the password for either the group or programs. I can't use or even delete them!

Although there's a dire warning in the *Getting Started* manual about recording the password for future reference, things are not at all that bleak. To find out the password for the group, use the View function in DOS SHELL to view file DOS\SHELL.MEU. It contains the passwords in ASCII directly after the name of the group. For example, if your group name was Word Processing, you'll see the password for this group shortly after the text "Word Processing" in the file.

To see the password for any program in the Group, View the menu file for the Group. The menu file has the same name as the Group filename with the extension .MEU. For example, if the Group Filename is WORDPRO, the menu is called WORDPRO.MEU. The password for the program is shortly after the text for the Title of the program.

Needless to say, this type of password protection will deter only the most inexperienced "crackers."

How can I get to command prompt mode from the DOS SHELL? Can I execute any DOS command in that mode?

To get to command prompt mode, just choose the command prompt mode from the Main Menu in DOS SHELL. This will temporarily terminate DOS SHELL operation and allow you to enter any number of DOS commands or to execute any number of programs. To get back to the Shell, enter EXIT after the DOS prompt.

Another way to get to command prompt mode is by pressing F3 (or select Exit and then Exit Shell). In this mode you'll have to enter DOSSHELL to re-enter the shell:

```
C:\>dosshell
```

There's really not a great deal of difference between one approach and the other.

I'm using commands in the command prompt mode, but find that the descriptions in the "Using DOS" manual are scanty. Where can I find additional information?

The best place for complete information on DOS commands is in the *Command Reference Manual*, available directly from IBM or from authorized computer stores. This is a 318-page publication that has an alphabetical listing of all DOS commands with detailed descriptions of each command. There is no further information in this manual relating to redirection of input/output, system configuration, batch files, code page switching, EDLIN, or the DOS SHELL, however. Those subjects are covered quite well in the "Using DOS" manual.

Another manual for advanced programmers also is available from some IBM authorized computer stores; It is the DOS Technical Reference Manual. This manual is primarily concerned with material of interest to programmers who are developing programs for IBM PC compatible systems.

All manuals should apply with few changes to MS-DOS 4.X running on non-IBM systems.

Is it possible to delete DOS functions that are seldom used to create a "bare-bones" DOS diskette that will run on a system without hard disk?

DOS modules now take up about 1.2M bytes of disk space. However, some modules are never used and others are used infrequently. For example, users without a hard disk will never use FDISK.COM; users with a hard disk will use it only when a hard disk is to be partitioned. Here are some guidelines for deletions:

• NEVER use your original DOS diskette; always make copies.
• A "bootable" disk must include the FORMAT /S options: two hidden files and COMMAND.COM.
• A file named after a DOS function followed by the extensions .COM or .EXE is required if you want that function. For example, DISKCOMP.COM implements the DOS DISKCOMP command and MEM.EXE implements the MEM command.
• Files with the .MOS extension are mouse drivers; delete if you have no mouse.
• Delete all SHELL.* files if you will not use DOS SHELL.
• Delete BASIC.COM, BASICA.COM, or GWBASIC.COM if you do not do BASIC programming.

- All files with obvious functions that do not exist on your system can be deleted: EGA. CPI, LCD. CPI, VDISK.SYS, etc.
- Experiment; if deleting a file causes a "File not found" error message, add it back in.

Are there any special things I need to do in DOS to connect my modem? I'm not having much luck with using a new modem in DOS 4.0. Do I need to use the MODE command?

That depends. Typical *external* modems connect to the communications port COM1, although they also could connect to communications port COM2.Connection is made with a serial connector cable. A connection also is made via a modular phone plug to the telephone line. Another connection is made to a low-voltage transformer that plugs into the wall socket. An *internal* modem plugs into a board slot on your system and has just the modular phone jack connection.

Normally, communications programs such as ProComm do all of the software work for you. You do not need to use the DOS MODE command. Such programs usually work in conjunction with a *Hayes compatible* modem. Is your modem Hayes compatible? (Most are.)

If you have a Hayes compatible modem and a proven communications program, the problem probably lies in setting internal DIP switches or jumper blocks in your modem. Look at the instruction manual that came with the system to verify that everything is set properly.

I get an "Access denied" message when I attempt to delete one of my subdirectories.

You probably have one or more files in your subdirectory that have not been deleted. DOS assumes if you have *any* files in the subdirectory that you want to save them and will not delete the subdirectory, which is a major step. Use the Select All function in the DOS SHELL to mark all files in the subdirectory. Then use the Delete function to delete the files. Now you can delete the subdirectory without any problem.

You'll also get the message if your subdirectory has one or more *subdirectories* that have not been deleted. To delete a subdirectory may involve going down several levels of subdirectories to delete all files and lower-level subdirectories before the higher-level subdirectory can finally be deleted.

I see in the "Using DOS" manual that there is a disk compare command. Do I need to compare two disks after a disk copy to make certain that the data has been copied correctly? How often is the data bad?

The DISKCOMP will compare two diskettes that have the same format, for example, two 720K 3.5-inch diskettes. Data is compared as it appears physically on the diskette and not on a file by file basis as in the COMP command.

Diskettes in the old days of microcomputers, ten years ago, had occasional errors. However, good quality diskettes today seldom have errors, so it's really not necessary to do a DISKCOMP after a disk copy from one diskette to another. It certainly wo*uldn't hurt*, but the chances of finding an error after a disk copy are probably one in one hundred diskettes.

It does pay to buy reasonable quality diskettes, however. Some bargain diskettes are a lot more prone to errors. Rather than a disk copy and subsequent disk compare for such disks, though, it's best to stick with good quality products such as 3M, Maxell, Kodak, Sony, and the many other reputable brands.

If you are experiencing disk errors every few hours of use and are using good quality diskettes, it may mean that your disk controller or disk drive needs repair.

I am running DOS SHELL from floppy disk. Should I include or not include the /TRAN startup option in the DOSSHELL.BAT file?

The /TRAN option makes the DOS SHELL a transient task; it stays in memory only as long as it is being executed. This is the normal mode when you are using DOS SHELL on a hard disk system since it can be easily reloaded from hard disk. If not in memory will create additional space for applications programs to run.

However, if you have DOS SHELL on a floppy, making DOS SHELL a *permanent* task by removing /TRAN keeps it in memory at all times. This uses additional memory space, but if you have a large enough memory, this is viable. The advantage of having DOS SHELL a permanent task is that you can remove the SHELL diskette and load another diskette in its place, either DOS utility programs or other programs or data you wish to access.

What is the EMS 4.0 Specification and how does it relate to DOS 4.0?

The EMS 4.0 specification is a memory standard implemented by Lotus, Intel, and Microsoft, sometimes referred to as "LIM". The original IBM PC and IBM PC-XT allowed only 640K bytes of user memory in a 1M byte addressing space (the remaining 384K bytes from 640K to 1M were used for graphics memory and device addresses). As programs such as Lotus 1-2-3 grew larger and required more memory, there was pressure to develop add-on memory boards to use more than the 640K bytes of user memory. The result was EMS 4.0 - Expanded Memory System 4.0. There are a number of manufacturers who now make add on boards to PC/XT compatible systems that follow this specification and increase the available memory by up to 8M bytes (8,388,608 bytes). One example is the Intel Above Board Plus.

Although programs such as Lotus 1-2-3 and Microsoft Windows recognize EMS, none of the previous DOS versions did. DOS 4.0 is the first DOS to provide EMS support and to allow certain DOS functions, such as virtual disks or disk buffers, to be located in the expanded memory area, freeing up the basic memory for larger user programs. DOS 4.0 recognizes both IBM expanded memory and non-IBM expanded memory that conforms to the EMS 4.0 specification.

What's the Meaning of the "File cannot be copied onto itself" error message?

Chances are you that you have done a copy to the current directory and not the one you were trying for. You *can* copy files from a directory or subdirectory into the same directory, but you must change the name before you do so. If DOS finds a file with the same name it will give you that error message. Try a slight variation on the name:

```
C:\>copy rawdata1.rec rawdata1.rc
```

If you're confused about what directory you're actually in, enter,

```
cd
```

and DOS will print out the current directory. Normally, though, the current directory is listed before the greater than prompt as well:

```
C:\SPRINT>
```

The first parameter in a COPY, XCOPY, or REPLACE is the *source* file, while the second is the *destination* file. Either parameter can use a path name, such as C:\SPRINT\PROBSOLV. Make certain that both paths are correct.

I keep getting a "File not found" message in trying to copy some files. What am I doing wrong?

The "File not found" message, followed by a file name, is displayed every time a DOS command specifies a file name that is not in the current directory. The *current* directory is the one that DOS is currently in. At any given time, there is a current directory for each disk in the system. The current directory is usually indicated by the DOS prompt path, which might look something like this:

```
C:\SPRINT\PROBSOLV>
```

In this example, the current path starts at drive C:, goes to the root directory (C:\), goes to a lower-level subdirectory in the root directory called SPRINT (C:\SPRINT), and then goes to a lower-level subdirectory in that directory called PROBSOLV (C:\SPRINT\PROBSOLV).

You can specify a complete path name and file name,

(C:\SPRINT\PROBSOLV\OPERFNFD.SPR)

for a DOS command,

```
C:type c:\sprint\probsolv
   \operfnfd.spr
```

or you can specify the path *from* the current directory. If the current directory is C:\SPRINT, the equivalent of the above is:

```
C:\SPRINT>type probsolv\operfnfd.spr
```

If in doubt about where a file is, do a DIR of the directory or subdirectory you think the file is in, using the complete path and file name. If in doubt about the current directory, do a CD command.

I get a "General failure reading drive A" message on an application program diskette I'm trying to read. What's wrong?

This message usually means that the diskette in the drive is either blank (has never been formatted) or was formatted in a different way than is recognizable by an MS-DOS system. For example, a diskette used by an Apple IIGS computer system is unreadable in an MS-DOS system and will give this error message.

If the diskette is supposed to contain an application program, check to see that the label specifies a program that is IBM PC compatible. If you think you previously formatted the diskette and copied programs to it, perhaps you mislabeled it or did not complete the format process.

How can I get immediate help without having to wade through pages of documentation?

You can in DOS SHELL, very easily. Press the F1 key at any time to get an on-screen display of "Help" data. See Figure 9. Use the PgUp and PgDn keys to scroll through the help text, which may cover many pages. The help text covers the item you have selected at the time, providing information on the basic function, formats, and keys.

If you must use the documentation, see the list of error messages in the "Using DOS 4.0" manual. It's fairly complete and provides action to take to clear up the error, sometimes arcane, but often helpful.

Also, you might consider buying the "Command Reference Manual" for DOS 4.0. It has an alphabetized listing of all DOS commands with formats and descriptions.

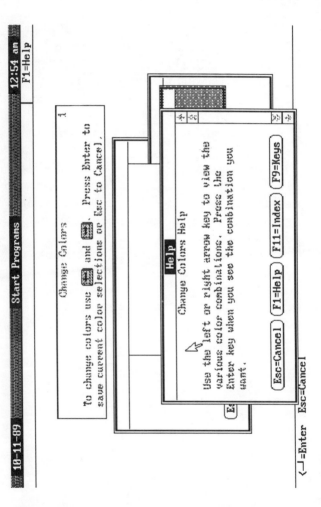

Figure 9

How can I tell if a file is a program file or a data file?

Program files have two extensions, either .COM or .EXE. Either type can be run simply by typing the name, with or without extension, in command prompt mode, or by selecting the file in DOS SHELL and opening (running) it.

.COM files are an image of the program as it existed when the program file was created. It stays in one place in memory.

.EXE files require a more elaborate loading procedure.

A file with the extension .BAT is a batch file. This is also an "executable" file started by typing the name with or without extension. However, the batch file is a series of DOS commands which are acted upon by the DOS command processor. The batch file may contain lines which cause .COM or .EXE files to be executed.

The Display Files option in the DOS SHELL in an EGA or CGA graphics system shows an icon opposite each file listing. An icon representing a page of text with the upper right corner turned indicates a non-executable file. An oval icon indicates a .COM, .EXE, or .BAT file. There is no corresponding notation for the DOS SHELL text screen.

I don't have enough memory to run some programs. I get either a "Program too big to fit in memory" or a "Not enough memory to continue" error message.

Because of a trend for larger and larger programs, total installed memory probably should be at least 512K to 640K for a viable system.

However, there are ways to get additional memory. First, you may have to get rid of virtual disks; they are notorious memory hogs. Delete any VDISK line from your CONFIG.SYS file (see "Startup, Modifying CONFIG.SYS").

Each disk buffer requires about 532 bytes. Reduce the BUFFERS parameter in the CONFIG.SYS file to a size small enough that a given program still runs (try BUFFERS=3).

Delete unneeded device drivers from your CONFIG.SYS file. For example, you may be loading a mouse driver that is not used in the application.

You may have to eliminate DOS SHELL by running in command prompt mode. Delete the DOSSHELL line from the AUTOEXEC.BAT file (see "Startup, Modifying AUTOEXEC.BAT ").

If these options don't do it, you may have to add additional memory. This is easy, but not inexpensive for a 80286 or 80386 system. Systems using an 8088 or 8086 have a 640K user memory limit, but this can be extended by an expanded memory board such as the Intel Above Board. DOS 4.0 supports both expanded and extended memory (80286 and 80386 systems).

Whenever I load and run a certain applications program from diskette and attempt to execute DOS commands in DOS prompt mode, I get an "Incorrect DOS version" error message.

You can verify what version of DOS is on a diskette by entering the command:

```
C:\>ver
```

in command prompt mode. You may find that the version is an earlier DOS version that does not include updated DOS commands. If this is the case, you can update your diskette to DOS version 4.X by the SYS command in command prompt mode. Load DOS 4.X and put the diskette to be updated in drive A:. Now enter,

```
C:\>sys c:\dos a:
```

to update the two system hidden files IBMBIO.COM and IBMDOS.COM (or their equivalent on MS-DOS) to the diskette to be updated.

After this update, copy the COMMAND.COM file from the DOS 4.X disk (assumed to be in directory C:\DOS) to the diskette to be updated. You should now be able to load and execute DOS 4.X from the updated diskette.

In attempting to do an XCOPY I get the error message "Invalid switch." What's happening?

Switches are options that are added to a DOS command. They are usually a single letter following a slash character. For example, the command:

```
C:\>xcopy a:*.spr c:\sprint\probsolv
   /m /d:7-15-89
```

uses two switches. The switch /m means copy a file whose archive bit is set, and /d:7-15-89 means copy a file whose date is the same or later than 7-15-89.

This error message indicates you entered a switch that is not valid for the DOS command or that the format of the switch is incorrect. For example, you might have entered,

```
C:\>xcopy a:*.spr
c:\sprint\probsolv
   /m /d7-15-89
```

leaving off a colon in the /d: switch.

Check the DOS command to see that the switch is valid and that the switch format is correct.

I'm attempting to run a word processing program, but I get the error message "No more files." What's wrong?

The CONFIG.SYS file determines the system configuration - the general parameters that DOS follows in using files and devices. One of the parameters, specified in a CONFIG.SYS line such as,

```
FILES=8
```

specifies the maximum number of open files that an application program can use. A word processor, for example, might require a file to read, a file to write, a font file, and two temporary files, a total of five files. Other applications programs might require 12 files to be opened at the same time. Since each open file requires additional memory, there must be a balance between the number of FILES and practical use. If the number specified in the FILES line is less than is actually required, though, DOS will respond with the error message above.

To correct, change the CONFIG.SYS file by adding additional files (see "Startup, Modifying CONFIG.SYS"). If the memory can support it, as many as 255 files can be opened at once. A more reasonable number, however, is 12.

I'm not sure what the PATH does in the AUTOEXEC.BAT file. Is it also used in command prompt mode?

The PATH command establishes a path that DOS searches for files. The directories on disk are arranged in a tree-like structure. At any given time, there is a *current directory* that is in force. Entering a program name in command prompt mode will start that program, *provided* that it is in the current subdirectory. DOS will search only the current directory for the program in the absence of any other path.

The PATH command, however, establishes other paths for DOS to follow in searching for the program. If a,

```
C:\>path c:\dos
```

command is entered, DOS will look for the FORMAT program in the current subdirectory and then in the C:\DOS subdirectory. Since DOS programs are used all the time from many different current directory locations, a path to DOS programs is very useful.

However, you also may execute other paths to follow to find a program:

```
C:\>path c:\dos; c:\sprint;
   c:\datacom
```

The command above establishes three paths for the search.

You can redefine PATH in the AUTOEXEC.BAT file for your own often-used subdirectories. When a path exists, only the program name need be given in the DOS SHELL Commands for Group/Program selection.

I visited a friend and instead of the normal DOS prompt, C:\>, his system used Hello, Jim:. How was this possible?

Easy. Use the command prompt command PROMPT to set a new DOS prompt. The format DOS SHELL creates is,

```
PROMPT $P$G
```

in which P stands for the current value of the default drive and G stands for the > character. The $ character is used to separate each new command string.

Other commands that can be used are $T (time), $D (date), $V (DOS version number), $N(default drive letter), $L (< character), $B (| character), $Q (the = character), $H (backspace character), $E (escape character), and $- (new line). Any text can be entered interspersed with the commands (except for $), so the command,

```
C:\>prompt Hello, Jim, the time is
   $t:
```

would change the prompt to:

```
Hello, Jim, the time is 11:12:30.58:
```

Use PROMPT alone without any characters to reset the prompt to NG (default drive followed by > character).

113

What do I do with READ.ME files that seem to be on every software package I buy?

You can read them easily by using the View File option in the DOS SHELL or by the command prompt command:

```
C:\>type read.me | more
```

The command above allows you to read them a screen at a time. You also may print them by the DOS SHELL Print option or by,

```
C:\>type read.me>prn
```

in command prompt mode.

READ.ME files usually are last minute notes (or the last six month's notes) that the software or hardware manufacturer has not been able to include in his printed documentation. They sometimes contain useful, sometimes vital notes that will help you get the software or hardware running correctly.

Sometimes the READ.ME file is named README or README. DOC, but the usage is the same.

When merging READ.ME files on the same directory, you may accidentally erase a prior information file with the same name. You may want to rename the files with unique extensions or different format to prevent this; try something like README. MS or READMEMS. TX1.

Can I get a program to run automatically, without having to enter responses from the keyboard? I have a program that takes the same responses each time it's run.

Yes, this is known as *redirecting input*. It can be done in the command prompt mode and works for short programs that don't require a long list of elaborate responses. For example, suppose you have a short program called RE-PORT1 that prints the following prompts and requires three responses:

```
Enter your name:
Enter your ID number:
Type of list you need (Daily (D),
Weekly (W)):
```

Every time you run the program, you reply with "Pascal, Bernie," "333-555," and "W;" the program then prints out a weekly report.

Make up an ASCII file (see "Files, Short ASCII") called RESPONSE (or any other name) containing these three lines:

```
Pascal, Bernie
333-555
W
```

You can then run the file automatically in command prompt mode by:

```
C:\>report1 <response
```

This line also can be incorporated in a batch file or Program Startup Command under DOS SHELL (see "Batch Files and PSCs, What are PSCs?").

I have a program that provides a printed report, but on the screen. Is there any way to capture the screen output into a file I can process with my word processor?

Yes, there is an easy way in command prompt mode. As an example, suppose your program is called REPORT3 and that it prints three reports on the screen. In loading the program, you can use a redirection symbol > and a file name to capture all output going to the screen. Suppose you want to capture the output in a file called TEXTOUT. TXT. You would say:

```
C:\>report3 >textout.txt
```

The program would run as usual, but any screen output also would be stored in file TEX-TOUT. TXT. The TEXTOUT. TXT file could now be processed by your word processor, assuming that it is capable of working with ASCII files, as most are.

Using two > symbols *appends* new output to an existing file or creates a new file if none exists. This way new text output can be added to an existing file:

```
C:\>report3 >>textout.txt
```

However, any time a single > is used, an existing file will be destroyed, so be careful not to use the > character when you mean >>.

This procedure does not work on all programs, especially those that have their own *screen drivers* and bypass DOS.

Is there any difference between the slash that looks like this \ and the slash that looks like this /?

Yes, a great difference. Use the \ slash only as a separator between directories. Every time DOS sees that type of slash, it assumes you are talking about a directory or subdirectory. An example is C:\DOS\FORMAT.COM which refers to the FORMAT.COM file in the DOS subdirectory in the C: drive.

The / slash is used for *switches*. Switches are options in command prompt lines, such as FORMAT A: /S, which formats the diskette in drive A and then puts system files onto the diskette. The /S stands for the system file option. (See "Operations, Invalid Switch.")

I'm trying to do an MD command to create a directory, but I'm getting an "Unable to create directory message".

This error can occur for several reasons. First, make certain the directory name you are using is a valid directory name. It must have one to eight characters, no extension (no . XXX portion), no spaces, and cannot have the symbols ."/\[]:*<>|+=;,?. It also cannot be one of the system reserved names - CLOCK$, CON, AUX, COM1, COM2, COM3, COM4, LPT1, PRN, LPT2, LPT3, or NUL.

If the name is all right, then check to see if the directory name already exists or if there is a file by that name in the directory. Use another name if it does.

If you're using the absolute form of the path for the MD, such as,

```
C:\>md c:\datacom\pccomm\function
```

make certain the higher-level directory names exist. In this example, DATACOM and PCCOM must exist.

Finally, if you're attempting to add the directory to the root directory, it may be full at 112 entries. Use another level or delete some of the entries (other subdirectories may have any number of entries).

Where can I go to get specialized help in running DOS in my PC compatible system? I have some annoying problems relating to display of characters on the screen and disk files which nobody at my computer store seems to know anything about. The system runs fine on DOS 3.3.

First of all, read "Startup, DOS 4.0 Corrections" if you are using PC-DOS and not MS-DOS. You must start with as bug-free a version of DOS as possible if you have not already done so.

There are so many combinations of systems and boards that it's impossible to cover all problems in a single book, much less a book of this size. There are two excellent places to try to get answers, however. First is your local computer club. Many clubs in major cities have hundreds of members and there's likely to be a member who has a system similar to yours who can provide an answer to your problem. A second source of information is one of the major data communication services such as CompuServe or Prodigy. Via modem, you can leave a message describing your problem in a *Special Interest Group* (SIG) dedicated to PC systems. Other members who are familiar with that particular problem are always glad to help.

The examples given in DOS documentation all seem to be in upper case (all capitals). However, I notice that lower case (small letters) seem to work just as well in most cases. Is it OK to use lower case?

Normally, you'll have the Caps Lock *off* when using the keyboard, pressing shift for upper case, just as on a typewriter. You may enter commands and parameters in upper case if you'd like, but it's just as valid to use lower-case commands and save some keystrokes. There are virtually no commands that will not work with lower-case characters. Text for group titles and help and text for program titles and help in DOS SHELL look better in upper and lower case, of course, but that's just an aesthetic consideration.

I'm having trouble running DOS under expanded memory in my system. How do I resolve it?

This is a question that cannot be answered easily in a single page in this book. IBM's "Using DOS 4.0" discusses the matter in eight pages and doesn't scratch the surface. Here are some tips to consider, however.

First of all, make certain that you have the 4.01 version of DOS. The DOS 4.00 version contains bugs relating to expanded memory support. Possibly DOS 4.01 will solve your problems (see "Startup, DOS 4.00 Corrections").

Next, if you have non-IBM expanded memory, it must conform to the LIM EMS 4.0 memory specification (see "Operations, EMS 4.0 Specification). DOS will not support expanded memory in other types of systems.

If you use the DOS expanded memory drivers XMA2EMS.SYS and XMAEM.SYS in a 80386 system, XMAEM.SYS must be installed before (must appear before) XMA2EMS.SYS in your CONFIG.SYS file.

If you have non-IBM expanded memory, try using the EMS memory drivers that came with the hardware, in place of the XMA2EMS.SYS or XMAEM.SYS drivers. Although both the IBM drivers and the non-IBM drivers should support the memory, there may be minor differences in the drivers.

How large should VDISK be in expanded or extended memory? And should I use the /E or /X option?

Use the /E option for VDISK if you have *extended* memory. Extended memory is found on 80286 or 80386 systems. Use the /X option for expanded memory. Expanded memory is found on IBM PC or IBM PC-XT compatible systems that use an EMS 4.0 memory expansion such as the Intel Above Board.

In either case, you can allocate from one to many virtual disks (ram disks) in the additional memory. You may want to experiment to find out whether a single large virtual disk or several smaller virtual disks work best in your application.

In general, make the virtual disks as large as necessary. If you have 4M bytes of additional memory, for example, there's no reason not to make the virtual disk 4096K bytes (4M bytes) with 512-byte sectors and 512 directory entries as in the CONFIG.SYS line:

```
DEVICE=VDISK.SYS 4096 512 512 /E
```

You'll have to use one DEVICE line for each virtual disk used; you'll also have to modify the LASTDRIVE line in the CONFIG.SYS file to accommodate all required virtual drives plus physical drives. (If in doubt, use LASTDRIVE=Z.)

I noticed in the AUTOEXEC.BAT file and in several commands that there is a verify mode for disk writes. Evidently, checks are made after disk writes to verify the data. Shouldn't VERIFY ON be included in the AUTOEXEC.BAT file and verify options be used in commands such as XCOPY as a double check on writing data?

You can if you wish, but disk operations will be slowed down considerably - probably about 60%. IBM recommends VERIFY OFF be used in the AUTOEXEC.BAT file because of the extra disk overhead. The data are read and verified after each write.

As stated elsewhere in this book, disk operations are extremely good and errors are infrequent unless you are using bargain diskettes. For this reason, VERIFY OFF can be used in the AUTOEXEC.BAT and in command options without problems. If you are getting disk errors more often than every few weeks and are using reasonable quality diskettes, there's a good likelihood that your disk controller or disk drives may have some problems.

Operations, When Should I Use Command Prompt Mode?

What's the purpose of command prompt mode? It seems as if I can do everything just fine from the DOS SHELL.

Yes, you can do just about everything from the DOS SHELL. The DOS SHELL provides operations that are hard to implement in command prompt mode, such as the ability to do a system file list of the entire disk in alphabetical or other order. However, operating in the command prompt mode sometimes may be more efficient. For example, read "Files, Renaming Many" to see how a group of files can be renamed automatically and in a few seconds, when the rename operation in the DOS SHELL would take ten to fifteen minutes.

The command prompt mode probably is best for operations such as this example, where it's simply faster. The ideal case would be to remain in the DOS SHELL for most operations but be familiar enough with the command prompt mode to make your overall operations more efficient.

Chapter 8

Printers

Printers, Garbage Printed

When I attempt to print out some of my word processing files using the DOS print function in the SHELL, I get some text, but a lot of garbage characters.

Your word processor probably uses special characters that cause destructive screen actions or print as garbage. Characters represented by decimal bytes 32 through 127 are *printable* characters. They display or print as:

```
(space) !"#$%&'()*+,-. /
0123456789:;<=>?@ABCDEFGHIJKLMNOPQRSTUVWXYZ
[\]^_`abcdefghijklmnopqrstuvwxyz{|}~
```

Characters represented by decimal bytes 128 through 255 are in the *extended character set*; they display or print as:

```
á  í  ó  ú  ñ  Ñ  ª  º  ¿  ⌐  ¬  ½  ¼  ¡  «  »
░  ▒  ▓  │  ┤  ╡  ╢  ╖  ╕  ╣  ║  ╗  ╝  ╜  ╛  ┐
└  ┴  ┬  ├  ─  ┼  ╞  ╟  ╚  ╔  ╩  ╦  ╠  ═  ╬  ╧
╨  ╤  ╥  ╙  ╘  ╒  ╓  ╫  ╪  ┘  ┌  █  ▄  ▌  ▐  ▀
α  β  Γ  π  Σ  σ  μ  τ  Φ  Θ  Ω  δ  ∞  φ  ε  ∩
≡  ±  ≥  ≤  ⌠  ⌡  ÷  ≈  °  •  ·  √  η  ²  ■
```

Some characters represented by decimal bytes 0 through 31 also may display on the screen, but some of them cause disruptive screen actions.

Word processing files may contain all byte values since they can process screen displays. However, the special codes in word processing files may cause completely different actions in DOS. There is no standardization between DOS actions and the word processing actions.

What this means in essence is that you cannot always print or display word processing files correctly, except in the word processing application program.

Whenever I try to print the screen in graphics mode, my printer shows garbled printing instead of a screen image. I'm certain that I'm using the DOS GRAPHICS command properly.

Unfortunately, PC-DOS in IBM equipment supports only IBM sanctioned printers such as the IBM 4201 Proprinter. Other MS-DOS versions may support different printers; refer to your MS-DOS manual for this information. Printers are not standardized in regard to control code sequences. Many printers emulate IBM printers, such as the Proprinter, while others do not. Emulation usually is enabled by DIP switches on the printer. If your printer is not an IBM printer on a PC-DOS system, is not supported by your MS-DOS system, or cannot emulate an IBM model supported by DOS, you will not be able to perform the screen print, even though you have executed the DOS GRAPHICS command and pressed the Shift key followed by the PrtSc key.

A special DEVICE driver would have to be programmed to support your printer, and this is not a trivial task. You may find such a driver in public domain software (bulletin boards, swap meets, and the like) if your printer is a very popular model such as the Hewlett-Packard LaserJet. Also, graphics processing programs such as Logitech's PaintShow often include a built-in screen capture and print capability for a wide range of printers and graphics screen types (CGA, EGA, and VGA).

My printer needs to be initialized by an escape code sequence. Every time I turn on the printer power, I must send a string of characters. Is there any way to do this automatically?

Some non-IBM printers require an initialization sequence. For example, some Tandy printers must be sent codes to prevent double line spacing. It also may be convenient to have a simple procedure to set a font or printer mode.

One way to do this is as follows:

Include file BASICA.EXE (sometimes called BASIC.EXE or GWBASIC.EXE in non-IBM systems) in the directory containing AUTOEXEC.BAT. Now create a batch file for the function to be set. For example, suppose that landscape mode is to be set in the LaserJet by the sequence Ec&l1O (Ec is decimal 27). An obvious choice for the file name is LANDSCAP.BAT. The file will contain:

```
basica<landscap.txt
```

Create a second file called LANDSCAP.TXT. It will contain:

```
lprint chr$(27)+"&l1O";
```

Include the line,

```
landscap
```

in the AUTOEXEC file. Now every time the system is restarted, the control code sequence Ec&l1O will be sent to the printer to set landscape mode. The same procedure may be followed to create any number of batch files for other printer functions. Set the function by starting the batch file at any time.

Whenever I print a file from DOS I lose characters at the end of the line.

When the DOS SHELL does a print of a selected file or when a PRINT or TYPE to PRN is done in command prompt mode, DOS does not format the lines. No carriage return/line feed characters are sent until the physical line end, which may be hundreds of characters. If your printer is not set up to do an "end of line wrap," all characters after a certain position - usually 80 - will be lost. If your printer has end of line wrap, characters are wrapped around and printed on a second line.

Most printers do have provision for automatic end of line wrap. Setting the printer usually involves a DIP switch setting or transmission of a special escape code sequence to the printer. For example, on the Hewlett-Packard LaserJet series, the special string Ec&s0C (where Ec is a value of decimal 27) must be sent to the printer to enable end of line wrap each time the printer is powered up.

See "Printers, Initializing" for information on how to initialize your printer automatically on system startup.

Is there any way I can get a running printout of what I see on the screen?

Yes, under certain conditions. There are three types of screen printouts, Graphics Screen Print, Print Entire Screen, andPrintLines. In text mode, as for example, in command prompt mode, you can print the entire screen by pressing the Shift key followed bythe PrtSc key. After the screen is printed, no further printing occurs. A graphics screen can be printed,provided you have used the GRAPHICS command to load a special graphics print driver (see"Printers, Graphics Screen Garbage"). Text and graphics screens are printed in either command prompt mode or under the DOS SHELL.

The third form of screen printing is disabled in DOS SHELL but works in command prompt mode. By pressing the Ctrl key followed by the PrtSc key, every line entered or displayed will be printed. The printing will continue over as many pages as you wish. It is turned off by pressing Ctrl and PrtSc again. However, just as DOS SHELL disables this type of printing, other programs also will not allow it. Some programs have their own screen drivers and do not go through DOS screen drivers. In this case, the Print Lines mode will not be detected.

I've been using MODE LPT1: 80,6,P in DOS 3. 3 so that DOS "retries" when printing. If I don't do this, DOS responds with a "Printer error" message. What is the setting in DOS 4.0?

Printer timeout errors occur on some printers that don't respond quickly enough when DOS asks if they are ready for the next character. Some older printers may be in the process of moving the head (as on carriage returns) or performing other operations that take a long time in comparison to computer processing. In DOS 3. 3, the P option allowed DOS to retry the printer to avoid error messages.

The MODE LPT1: format has been changed somewhat in DOS 4.0. There are still the columns, lines, and retry options, but they now are listed as the parameters LINES, COLS, and RETRY. RETRY has three values, E (network use), B (return busy status), and R (return ready status). The option corresponding to the P option is:

```
C:\>mode lpt1: cols=80 lines=6 retry=B
```

Use MODE in command prompt mode to get a listing of the current mode settings for LPT1:, LPT2:, LPT3:, and CON:.

Reset retry by entering MODE LPT1: without parameters.

How can I do a screen print of a graphics screen? And how can I tell which screen is a graphics screen? Is DOS able to tell the difference and print the proper way?

To answer your last question first, DOS is able to tell when a text screen and when a graphics screen is enabled, and prints either text characters or graphics characters. However, this is assuming that a special graphics print driver has been loaded.

The general procedure for loading the graphics print driver is to include it in your AUTOEXEC.BAT file (see "Startup, Modifying AUTOEXEC.BAT File"). However, the DOS GRAPHICS command also can be used in command prompt mode at any time.

To use GRAPHICS, your system must have an IBM-supported printer such as an IBM 4201 Proprinter or a printer that can emulate an IBM printer. (See "Printers, Graphics Screen Garbage" for what happens if you do not have such a printer.) The various GRAPHICS options are described in "Using DOS 4.0." Associated with the GRAPHICS. COM graphics print driver is a second file, GRAPHICS. PRO. This is a "profile" file describing the printer and is created during the SELECT program process when you specify the type of printer. Both GRAPHICS.COM and GRAPHICS.PRO must be in the same directory when you load GRAPHICS.COM in AUTOEXEC.BAT or command prompt mode.

I know that I can get a listing of all subdirectories and files contained within them from the shell. However, I'd like a hard copy. Is there any way to get one?

The easiest way to get a complete listing of all subdirectories and files within them on a disk is to use the TREE command in command prompt mode. For a complete listing of a hard disk, press the Ctrl key followed by the PrtSc key, change the directory to the root, and enter the TREE command with the /F option and printer output:

```
C:\>cd c:\
C:\>tree /f >prn
```

You'll see a complete listing of the root directory, all subdirectories, and all files within the root and subdirectories displayed on the screen and printed at the same time. See Figure 10. Your printer should be capable of printing line segment characters (see "Printers, Setting Graphics Screen Print") or use the /A option:

```
C:\>cd c:\
C:\>tree /f /a >prn
```

```
        LETTERHD
        TIMECARD.SPR

  TEXT
        CP499NET
        TESTPRNT.SPR
        WC.EXE
        BLOCK
        DJ122988.RAI
        BG122988.BG

  TANDY
        LL011489.RS

  DOS4POSC
        WC.EXE

    TIFFIGS
        FIG0101.TIF
        FIG0102.TIF
        FIG0301.TIF
        FIG0303.TIF
        FIG0304.TIF
        FIG0305.TIF
        FIG0306.TIF
        FIG0308.TIF
        FIG0309.TIF
        FIG0311.TIF
        FIG0315.TIF
        FIG0316.TIF
        FIG0317.TIF
        FIG0318.TIF
        FIG0319.TIF
```

Figure 10

Chapter 9

Programs

Programs, Bad Command or File Name

I'm just starting to add groups and programs within the groups to the DOS SHELL. However, when I try to start some of the programs after selecting the group and program, I get a "Bad command or file name" message. What's wrong?

This probably means that DOS was unable to locate the program. You must do more than simply enter the program name under Commands. Depending upon the way you installed DOS you are probably in a *subdirectory* called C:\DOS, at this point. If the program you are trying to start is not also in that subdirectory, DOS will not find it (unless a PATH exists; see "Operations, PATH").

The easiest way to ensure that DOS *can* find the program is to specify a complete path along with the file name. If the program is called WP.EXE and it is in a subdirectory called WORDPERF on hard disk C:, you'd have to enter the command,

```
c:\wordperf\wp
```

to start the program when selected (the .EXE extension on the filename WP does not have to be included). When the program is run, the current subdirectory will still be C:\DOS and that might cause problems in the program. To change to the WORDPERF subdirectory *and* start the program you'd need:

```
cd c:\wordperf ‖ wp
```

You may enter many other startup commands as well.

I'm confused about how the Group name,
filename for the group, and program title in a
group relate to the actual program file name.
Must any of them be the same?

The Group name can be any descriptive text
defining the main purpose of the group, such as:

```
Word Processing
Spreadsheets
C Programming Utilities
```

Blanks can be included and up to 37 characters, upper and lower case, can be used. The
Group title doesn't have to relate at all to the
programs in the group, although it can ("Spread-
sheets" might be retitled "Lotus", for example).

The filename for the group also is unrelated
to the programs in the group. It's simply a
filename that DOS uses to make a special menu
file with the extension .MEU for that group. If
you like, you can use the filename (without
extension) of the main program in the group.

The program title in a group also does not
have to relate to the actual program filename.
You can use any descriptive text you'd like of up
to 40 characters with blanks. A typical program
title might be "Borland's Sprint Word Processor."

The Commands field *does* tie in the program name to the program title. The simplest case would be a command to load and run the program, such as C:\SPRINT\SP. (See "Batch Files and PSCs,What Are PSCs?")

Occasionally when I run a certain program, the system appears to "lockup." Nothing that I do will bring operation back to normal. What's happening?

System lockup occurs for a variety of reasons. The program that you are running may have a bug (error) in it that causes the program to loop within itself continually. Software errors that cause this are less common than they once were, but still exist. Try pressing the Esc (Escape) key or the Ctrl key followed by the C key. Some programs look for these keys as a way to return control back to the program or operating system.

Another thing that causes system lockup is a hardware design error. This also may be essentially a software error if the hardware controller contains "firmware", a permanently recorded program within the hardware device.

Try to isolate under what circumstances the error occurs. If you can find the conditions under which the error repeats, you may be able to contact the hardware or software manufacturer's technical support department for assistance.

When system lockup occurs, pressing the Ctrl key, the Alt key, and the Del key simultaneously will reboot the system in a "warm start;" it's often not necessary to power down and then power up, although this may clear some extreme cases.

Programs, No Paths

I have an old program that I use all the time. Unfortunately, the program does not allow subdirectory paths, and I have to transfer files to the subdirectory in which the program resides to have the program recognize the files. Is there a way around this in DOS?

The SUBST command in command prompt mode allows you to substitute a drive specifier such as F: for any path. Executing a,

```
C:\>subst f: c:\wordpro\general
```

for example, equates path c:\wordpro\general to drive specifier F:. Thereafter, you can enter the new drive specifier F: when your program asks for the drive on which the files are located (if it does).

You can use any number of drive specifiers up to Z:. However, before you do this, you must change the LASTDRIVE command in your CONFIG.SYS file (see "Startup, Modifying CONFIG.SYS") to include the drive specifier used:

```
LASTDRIVE=F
```

Use the /D option to remove the substitution:

```
C:\>subst f: /d
```

Is it really necessary to add group and program passwords in the DOS SHELL Add Group and Add Programs functions? What passwords should be used?

If you're a single user operator of your DOS system and no one else has access to it, adding Group and Program passwords is definitely overkill and a nuisance in starting programs. In this case, don't even use them. However, password protection is there if you want it and it does come in handy in office or multiple user environments. Because there's a password both for the group and for programs in the group, you can allow any number of users access to a group, but prevent all programs in the group from being used.

Passwords for both Groups and Programs can be one to eight characters. It's best to choose the maximum number of random characters not related to birthdates, auto licenses, husband or wife's name, etc. Good examples are AJE4B9XI, 1MFAIHDO, and PQ6VFJJ3. There are about 6,550,000,000,000 passwords that can be made from eight characters, so the likelihood of someone stumbling onto your *random* password is almost nil.

Isn't there an easier way to start a program than displaying a group of files, selecting a program file, and then opening (starting) it?

Yes, you're missing a *very* easy way. The basic Command, File System, Change Colors, and DOS Utilities groups displayed in the Main Group under DOS SHELL can be expanded to include your own groups. For example, you might add several Word Processing groups, a Lotus 1-2-3 group, a Basic Compiler Group, a Backup Group, and others, as shown in Figure 11. You can then select your own group by moving the selection cursor. This action then displays the files in that group and you can move the selection cursor to a program (file) and load and start it automatically. The whole process takes a few seconds as opposed to dozens of seconds the other way.

First, you must add an item in the Main Group by using the Add in Group in the SHELL. You'll be prompted for title, filename, help text, and password. After the group is added, you can select that group and add programs to the group by selecting the Add function in Group, again being prompted, for title, commands, help text, and password. In the simplest case, you'll simply add a meaningful title and then add a command such as,

```
c:\sprint
```

for loading and running the program. (See "Batch Files and PSCs, What are PSCs?")

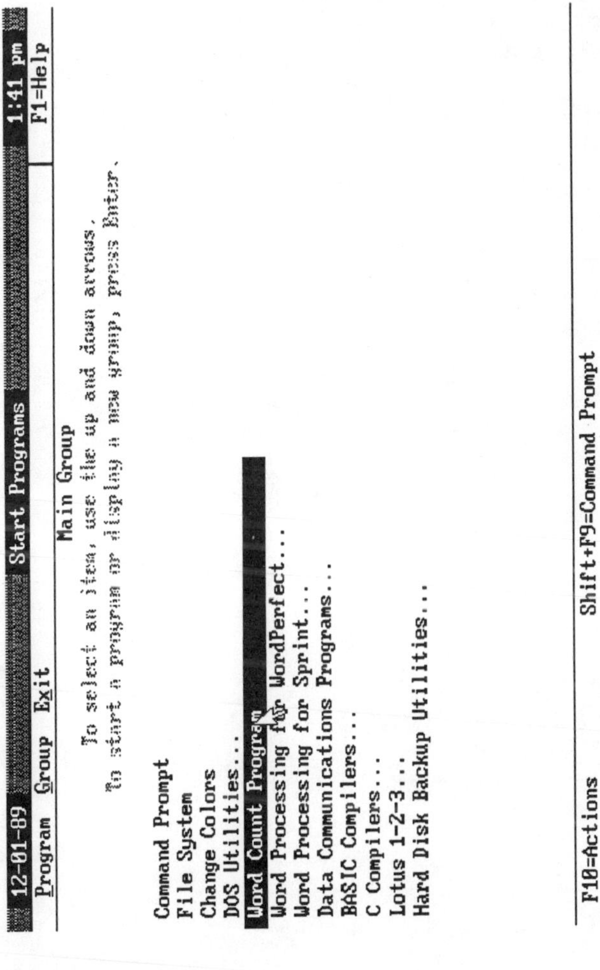

Figure 11

Chapter 10

Startup

Startup, Communications Port

What should be the settings for the communication port?

Read "Operations, Connecting Modem" if you want to know how to connect a modem for data communications.

If you are using a serial printer connected to a communications port, read "Printers, Serial."

Typical systems have one or two asynchronous communication ports, labeled COM1 or COM1 and COM2. If an application program doesn't set up the communication parameters, you can do it through the MODE COM1 DOS command. There are five parameters here, baud rate (BAUD), number of data bits (DATA), number of stop bits (STOP), and parity type (PARITY).

The baud rate is data transmission speed and is determined by the device. A serial printer may be able to run at 300, 600, or 1200 baud or more. Dividing the baud rate by 10 normally gives you the number of characters per second.

The number of data bits can be set to 5, 6, 7, or 8, but is usually 8, sometimes 7, and almost never 5 or 6.

The number of stop bits is 1, 1.5, and 2. Normally the number of stop bits is 1.

The parity type may be NONE, ODD, EVEN, MARK, or SPACE. Typically the parity is NONE, ODD, or EVEN in about that order.

A frequently used set of parameters is:

```
C:\>mode baud=1200 data=8 stop=1
parity=none
```

The MODE command can be used in the AUTOEXEC.BAT file or may be used in command prompt mode at any time.

I have PC-DOS version 4.01, but when I tried VER to get the version number, the command displayed "4.00." Do I have the wrong DOS version?

No, you have the right version. PC-DOS 4.01 displays version 4.00. The original release of the PC-DOS using the SHELL concept was PC-DOS 4.00. There were minor errors in this version relating to use of expanded memory (EMS) (see "Startup, DOS 4.0 Corrections"). These were partially corrected in temporary "patch" disks and finally incorporated into PC-DOS 4.01. IBM's policy in regard to version numbers is to change the second digit for more major changes. (However, MS-DOS 4.01 is correctly displayed by VER as "4.01.")

There may be additional releases of PC-DOS and these might be labeled 4.1, 4.2, and so forth.

I was using DOS 3.3. Are there any "gotchas" in DOS 4.0 - things that worked in DOS 3.3 but that do not work in DOS 4.0?

DOS 4.0 retains all of the advantages of DOS 3.3 and adds many new features. It's only in the new features that there may be some "gotchas".

Support of expanded memory has some bugs in the early version of DOS 4.00; get the revised 4.01 version. Use of expanded memory in general may be difficult. Application programs that use expanded memory may conflict with DOS usage and cause problems. High-speed interrupt processing with virtual disks in extended memory use may result in missed interrupts in certain cases.

The DOS SHELL provides a presentation manager-like approach to DOS functions. However, the memory required for DOS SHELL reduces the overall memory available for user programs.

New features have resulted in more and larger programs. The total disk space requirements for DOS have been increased. Users with smaller capacity disk drives may have to do more swapping or consolidation of programs onto a reasonable number of DOS diskettes.

You also will find that the formats for some commands have changed slightly, although most commands that existed in DOS 3.3 will have the same format.

I bought PC-DOS 4.0 and have had no problems with it. However, I understand there are "patches" to this version of DOS. Are they necessary? How can I obtain them?

Yes, there are patches to the original DOS 4.0 and we would advise getting them. DOS 4.0 contained programming errors (bugs) related primarily to expanded memory (EMS). If you are not using EMS, then you may not have seen any problems on your system. IBM released a DOS patch disk called a Corrective Service Diskette (CSD) to correct these errors, and then released a new version of DOS called 4.01 which incorporated the patches.

You sometimes can obtain the CSD from the dealer from which you purchased your DOS 4.0. Be sure to obtain all current CSDs.

At this time of writing, here are the CSD numbers and dates:

CSD UR22624 8/15/88
CSD UR24270 3/27/89
CSD UR25066 5/10/89

The first two CSDs are incorporated in PC-DOS 4.01. The third corrects problems relating to non-IBM EMS memory boards.

Can I use PC-DOS 4.X with my PC compatible?

That depends. If your PC compatible is a *true* compatible, you may find that PC-DOS 4.X will run correctly on your system. Systems such as Compaq are noted for being very compatible, although we can't guarantee that PC-DOS 4.X will run on all Compaq machines. There are a host of other systems, however, that are not perfectly compatible, ranging from moderately incompatible to almost compatible. The basic philosophy behind DOS 4.X was to provide a version for IBM systems and versions for other manufacturers. The other 4.X DOS versions are called *MS-DOS* instead of PC-DOS.

At this time of writing there is a Phoenix/ Microsoft MS-DOS version 4.01 available in some stores. However, even this version will not run on all systems. The most foolproof approach here is to wait until an authorized version of MS-DOS comes out for your system. If your system is from a manufacturer who will not release their own version of DOS and a generic MS-DOS does not run correctly, there is no solution to this problem.

I changed my CONFIG.SYS file for a device driver, but now I get an "Error in CONFIG.SYS line 9" when I reboot. What's wrong?

DOS isn't very specific about what the error in a CONFIG.SYS file consists of. The assumption is that if you just changed the CONFIG.SYS file, you'll have a good idea of the change causing the error. Look at the line number where the error occurred to see that it does correspond to your changed line. Do a,

```
C:\>type c:\config.sys
```

command in command prompt mode to see that the CONFIG.SYS file in general and the changed line in specific contain only printable text characters and not "odd" characters (such as a star or musical note). If the CONFIG.SYS file does contain such characters, you've probably changed the file using a word processor that does not output the file in ASCII. Redo CONFIG.SYS by the procedure in "Files, Short ASCII" in this case.

Make certain that the format of the CONFIG.SYS command line is correct with proper spelling, the proper number of parameters, and the proper range of parameter values.

When changing CONFIG.SYS, it's always best to keep the old file as CONFIG.BAK or a similar name so that you can restore the system to a working state!

In installation, what combination of the three functions and workspace should I choose?

Option number one (minimum function, maximum program work space) should be used for systems with minimum memory (on the order of 360K bytes). It generates a CONFIG.SYS file used in startup for a minimum number of buffers and drivers; for example, ANSI.SYS and FASTOPEN.EXE are not used.

Option number three (maximum function, minimum workspace) should be used for systems with maximum memory, such as 80286 or 80386 systems with extended memory or IBM PC/PC-XT compatible systems with expanded memory. It generates a CONFIG.SYS file with many buffers and drivers; for example, FASTOPEN.EXE, ANSI.SYS, and 25 disk buffers.

Option number two is a compromise for systems with about 640K bytes of memory. It generates BUFFERS=20 and FILES=8, and the ANSI.SYS, and FASTOPEN.EXE drivers in CONFIG.SYS.

All options generate an AUTOEXEC.BAT file that results in the DOS SHELL being loaded.

Like the other INSTALL options, the CONFIG.SYS and AUTOEXEC.BAT files can be changed at a later time. What you get is not absolute.

I have a single 5.25-inch diskette system without hard disk. How do I load DOS?

First, of course, you must install DOS on four 5.25-inch diskettes (see "Startup, Number of Diskettes for DOS"). These are labeled Startup, Shell, Working 1, and Working 2. The Startup diskette contains the main portion of DOS, but not the SHELL. The Shell diskette contains the SHELL program. The Working 1 and Working 2 diskettes contain utility programs such as FORMAT, FDISK, and MORE.

DOS always must be loaded using the Startup diskette. Insert it in drive A: and press the Ctrl key, the Alt key, and the Del key together and release.

Once DOS is loaded, you'll see the title message and the prompt:

A:\>

You now can run common DOS commands directly without having to load another disk. You can remove the diskette from drive A:, as a matter of fact. To run DOS SHELL, remove the Startup diskette and insert the Shell diskette. Enter:

A:\>dosshell

You now can perform the basic functions of DOS SHELL, but will not be able to perform Utility functions. To perform utility functions, you'll have to enter command prompt mode and load and execute utilities from one of the other three diskettes.

I have a dual 5.25-inch diskette system without hard disk. How do I load DOS?

Read "Startup, Loading DOS With One 360K Drive" to find out the basic steps in loading DOS from the A: drive. Having a second drive makes things a little easier than a one drive system. For one thing, you can setup a PATH (see "Operations, PATH") using both drives:

```
A:\>path a:\; b:\
```

This means that if a file is not found on drive A:, DOS will automatically search for it on drive B:.

Although the Utilities Group in DOS SHELL will be empty, you can add the disk copy, disk compare, backup, restore, and format functions by putting program modules DISKCOPY.COM, DISKCOMP.COM, BACKUP.COM, RESTORE. COM, and FORMAT.COM together on a single diskette in B: and then enter the proper PSC commands to define a utilities group. Suggested PSC commands are:

```
date [/t"Set Date and Time
Utility"/i"Enter new date ??-??-
??"/l"8"]‖time [/t"Set Date and
Time Utility"/i"Enter new time
hh:mm"/l"5"]‖pause
diskcopy [/t"Diskcopy Utility"/
```

```
i"Enter source and destination
drives."/p"Drives . ."/d"a: b:"/
r]‖pause
diskcomp [/t"Diskcomp Utility"/
i"Enter drive for comparison."/
p"Parameters . ."/d"a: b:"/
r]‖pause
backup [/t"Backup Utility"/i"Enter
source and destination drives."/
p"Parameters . ."/d"c:\*.* a: /s"/
r]‖pause
restore [/t"Restore Utility"/
i"Enter source and destination
drive."/p"Parameters . ."/d"a:
c:\*.* /s"/r]‖pause
format [/t"Format Utility"/i"Enter
drive to Format."/p"Parameters .
."/d"a: "/r]‖pause
```

How do I modify the AUTOEXEC.BAT file to include command lines required by some of my special-purpose hardware? Must I use EDLIN?

The AUTOEXEC.BAT file is executed automatically on system power on (cold start) or when the system is rebooted (warm start). It contains not only definitions required by DOS, but may cause execution of other programs, such as Sidekick or special drivers. For example, here is an AUTOEXEC.BAT command line that executes a special VGA graphics driver:

```
VEGA PURE ON
```

Various system add-on cards and software require command lines in the AUTOEXEC.BAT file, so it may be necessary to modify the AUTOEXEC.BAT text created by the DOS INSTALL program. To do so, use EDLIN, if you know the EDLIN commands. However, a better way is to use your own word processing program in pure text mode. Most word processors (WordPerfect, WordStar, Sprint, etc.) enable you to create a pure text (ASCII) file containing only text characters, carriage returns, and line feeds. AUTOEXEC.BAT files must be in this pure text mode, since DOS does not know how to interpret special control characters.

How do I modify the CONFIG.SYS file to include command lines required by some of my special-purpose hardware? Must I use EDLIN?

The CONFIG.SYS file is executed automatically on system power on (cold start) or when the system is rebooted (warm start). It contains general system definitions and information about system devices. For example, here is a CONFIG.SYS command line that specifies a special 3.5" disk driver in a PC-XT system:

```
DEVICE=DRIVER.SYS/d:1
```

Various system add-on cards and software require command lines in the CONFIG.SYS file, so it may be necessary to modify the CONFIG.SYS text created by the DOS INSTALL program. To do so, use EDLIN, if you know the EDLIN commands. However, a better way is to use your own word processing program in pure text mode. Most word processors (WordPerfect, WordStar, Sprint, etc.) enable you to create a pure text (ASCII) file containing only text characters, carriage return, and line feed. CONFIG.SYS files must be in this pure text mode as DOS does not know how to interpret special control characters.

I recently acquired some software on a disk from a friend. However, when I try to "boot the system," the screen shows "Non-system disk or disk error."

The diskette you've received probably doesn't have certain system files on it. To make a new diskette that will boot:

1. Boot DOS or enter DOSSHELL.

2. Select FORMAT from the DOS Utilities Menu or enter:

```
C:\>format a: /s
```

3. Load a new or reusable diskette into drive A: and follow the instructions for the FORMAT program to format your diskette with COMMAND.COM and the two hidden files IBMBIO.COM and IBMDOS.COM (similar files are used for MS-DOS).

4. Two drive system: Put the diskette you've received in drive A: and the newly formatted diskette in drive B:. Use the DOSCOPY to copy all the files on the diskette you've received to the newly formatted diskette. (Use COPY A:*.* B: in command prompt mode.)

5. One floppy drive, one hard disk:

a. Make a new directory anywhere on the hard disk (see "File, Subdirectory Format"). We'll call it C:\ROOT\NEW here.

    b. Copy from the original diskette to this new directory under the shell COPY or by COPY A:*.* C:\ROOT\NEW.

    c. Now copy all files from C:\ROOT\NEW to the newly formatted diskette in drive A:.

  6. The result is a disk that can be booted to initialize DOS, but contains all files from the original diskette.

I have a two floppy disk system. How many diskettes are required for DOS? Is it feasible to run DOS?

It's certainly possible to install DOS on diskettes in place of hard disks. Follow the instructions in the DOS INSTALL procedure to switch diskettes back and forth. You'll wind up with four diskettes for a system with 360K or 1. 2M byte 5.25-inch drives, two diskettes for a system with a 720K byte 3.5-inch drive, and one diskette for a system with a 1.44M byte 3.5-inch drive. The 1.44M byte drive system diskette holds the entire DOS. However, each of the other systems has a Startup diskette, containing the command prompt version of DOS and an additional one to three diskettes containing the SHELL and utility programs such as FORMAT and SORT.

The problem with having DOS on multiple diskettes is that you may have to continually insert a DOS diskette in the drive to obtain utility programs. This is not as much of a problem with a dual 1.44M byte drive system, but is most annoying with a single 360K byte drive system. Running in DOS SHELL is difficult, if not impossible, if disk swapping is required; you may have to run in command prompt mode without the shell.

One solution is to reduce the number of program modules required to as few disks as possible. (See "Operations, Condensed DOS Diskette.")

Can I put descriptive text in my CONFIG.SYS file?

Fortunately, you can. DOS 4.0 added a new REM command for CONFIG.SYS to enable you to do just that. The REM statement doesn't cause any action, but can denote what is happening. The REM statement doesn't even display during system startup. You can display the CONFIG.SYS file at any time by:

```
C:\>type c:\config.SYS
```

Here's a typical CONFIG.SYS file with remarks:

```
REM MOUSE VERSION
BREAK=ON
BUFFERS=20
FILES=8
LASTDRIVE=F
SHELL=C:\DOS\COMMAND.COM /P /E:256
DEVICE=C:\DOS\ANSI.SYS
INSTALL=C:\DOS\FASTOPEN.EXE
   C:=(50,25)
REM FOR SECOND HARD DISK
DEVICE=DRIVER.SYS/D:1
DEVICE=C:\GMOUSE.SYS
DEVICE=C:\DOS\VDISK.SYS 128 512 64
```

See "Startup, Modifying CONFIG.SYS" for information on how to insert REM lines.

Startup, Time Not Correct

I just setup and started using my system with DOS 4.0. However, the time displayed is not correct. What's the problem?

You must set the date and time by using the Set Date and Time option under Utilities in the DOS SHELL, or by using the DATE and TIME commands in command prompt mode. After you do that, DOS wil lmaintain the correct time and display it on the screen. Setting the correct date and time must be done after each "cold-start" -restarting the system after power has been turned off.

The exception to this is when your system has a built-in clock/calendar board. Such boards plug into the bus on the system motherboard or, in some cases, fit into a socket on the motherboard. (IBM-PC AT systems or compatibles have a built-in clock calendar.) They maintain the date and time by a self-contained clock similar to a digital wrist watch. If you have such a board and still are not getting the correct date and time, you may need to change the AUTOEXEC.BAT file to include a call to a special driver that reads the current date and time into the system on each power-up. Consult the manual for your clock/calendar board and see "Startup, Modifying AUTOEXEC.BAT."

In attempting to install DOS 4.0 on my system, DOS created an AUTOEXEC.400 file instead. I still have an AUTOEXEC.BAT file left over. How do I merge the two files?

If an AUTOEXEC.BAT file exists when the DOS SELECT program is run, DOS creates an AUTOEXEC.400 file in place of an AUTOEXEC.BAT file. It's up to you to compare the two files to determine the needed commands.

In general, keep the sequence and content of the AUTOEXEC.400 file, but merge other command lines from the existing AUTOEXEC.BAT file. If necessary, make a new path that combines all paths in both files, with the PATH from AUTOEXEC.400 first (usually PATH C:\DOS); use semicolons to separate each path. Unless you want to restart the system and bypass DOS SHELL, make the last line in the new AUTOEXEC.BAT file DOSSHELL, which will startup with the DOS SHELL.

Rename your original AUTOEXEC.BAT file to AUTOEXEC.BAK (or similar) so that you will have it to refer to later. Modify the AUTOEXEC.BAT file by following the procedure in "Startup, Modifying AUTOEXEC.BAT." Save the new AUTOEXEC.BAT file in the root directory of the startup drive. Reboot the system and see if all seems in order. If not, compare the new AUTOEXEC.BAT file with AUTOEXEC .BAK and AUTOEXEC. 400 and try again.

I attempted to install DOS 4.0 on my system, but DOS created a CONFIG. 400 file instead. I still have a CONFIG.SYS file left over. Some of the commands are different. How do I proceed?

If a CONFIG.SYS file exists when the DOS SELECT program is run, DOS creates a CONFIG.400 file in place of a CONFIG.SYS file. It's up to you to compare the two files and determine which commands are needed. Here are some guidelines.

BREAK should generally be ON. Set BUFFERS to the highest number found in either file. Use the FCBS line with the largest values found in either file. Set FILES to the highest number found in either file. Use the LASTDRIVE parameter providing the greatest number of drives. Keep the SHELL command line. Keep the CONFIG. 400 DEVICE line with ANSI. Use all DEVICE=DRIVER lines from both files. Keep the SHELL line from CONFIG.400. Use the INSTALL line from CONFIG.400.

Rename your original CONFIG.SYS file to CONFIG.BAK (or similar) so that you will have it to refer to later. Modify the CONFIG.SYS file by following the procedure in "Startup, Modifying CONFIG.SYS." Save the new CONFIG.SYS file in the root directory of the startup drive. Reboot the system and see if all seems in order. If not, compare the new CONFIG.SYS file with CONFIG.BAK and CONFIG.400 and try again.

What are the proper Review Selections for the INSTALL program in DOS installation? Is it all right to use the selections DOS makes?

The Review Selections in the DOS installation are used to construct lines in the CONFIG.SYS and AUTOEXEC.BAT files that DOS generates as part of the installation procedure. These two files can be modified easily after the DOS installation, so don't feel that you must make immediate decisions about the options at installation time (see "Startup, Modifying AUTOEXEC.BAT" and "Startup, Modifying CONFIG.SYS").

Code page switching is used primarily if you are a non-United States user. Extended display support usually is not necessary except for application programs using the ANSI screen codes. GRAPHTABL relates to code page switching. GRAPHICS print screen support can be bypassed if your printer is not IBM graphics printer compatible. Choose DOS SHELL if you'd like to operate from the DOS SHELL, which is usually the case. Choose virtual disk support if you'd like to install a RAM disk (simulated disk in memory). If in doubt, go with the DOS default values (press <ENTER>).

Startup, What Should be Used for Configuration Parameters?

What are the proper Configuration Parameters for the Install Program in DOS installation? Can the default values be used?

This menu in INSTALL sets values that are used to build a CONFIG.SYS file. The CONFIG.SYS file can be modified at a later time, so it's not critical to get the proper values at installation time. In fact, there are no *proper* values for some of the parameters.

BREAK normally is on to allow DOS to be interrupted more frequently by pressing the Ctrl key followed by the Break key. BUFFERS sets the number of disk buffers. Each buffer uses about 532 bytes; use fewer (typically three) for a system with little memory. FCBS refers to network file sharing, not used on most systems. FILES establishes the number of files that can be open at one time; most applications programs require only a few. LASTDRIVE must be increased alphabetically when a virtual disk or certain DOS commands are used. VERIFY should normally be OFF to make system disk operations faster (see "Operations, VERIFY").

Use the tab key (two left and right arrows) to get to the proper field and change as desired, or simply use the default values, which will work without problems.

What are the proper DOS SHELL Parameters for the INSTALL Program in DOS installation? Can the default startup options be used?

The DOS SHELL Parameters in DOS installation are used to construct a batch file that loads the DOS SHELL. This file can be changed easily at a later time to add or correct any startup options that were missed, so adding the proper startup options at installation time is not absolutely necessary. The, /MENU, /DOS, /PROMPT, /EXIT, /MAINT, /COLOR, /TRAN, /MEU:SHELL.MEU, /CLR:SHELL.CLR, /MUL, /SND, /SWAP and /DATE options are normal options that probably should be present on all shells for full capability. The /MOS:PCIBMDRV .MOS option loads the IBM mouse driver if you have such a device. If you have another type of mouse, see "Mouse, Installation in DOS." The /LF sets a mouse to left-handed operation (see "Mouse, Left-Handed"). The /COM2 allows a serial mouse to be used on the second serial port (leaving the first free for a modem). The /TEXT, /CO1, /CO2, and /CO3 options set text mode, EGA, VGA two-color, or VGA 16-color modes (see "Display, EGA. . ." and "Display, VGA. . .").

Add any options relating to your mouse or graphics mode by the arrow keys, Ins (insert), and Del (delete). Press <ENTER> when the line reads correctly. Here's a typical line:

```
@SHELLC  /MOS:PCMSDRV.MOS/CO3/COLOR/
TRAN/DOS/MENU/MUL/SND
/MEU:SHELL.MEU/CLR:SHELL.CLR/PROMPT/
MAINT/EXIT/SWAP/DATE
```

Chapter 11

Utilities

The BACKUP and RESTORE utilities in DOS work, but they are very slow and take many floppy diskettes! Isn't there a better way to backup my hard disk?

The BACKUP and RESTORE utilities under DOS are not very efficient compared to non-IBM products such as Fastback. If you do use BACKUP and RESTORE, realize that you don't have to back up the entire disk each time. Just back up those files that have changed after a specified date or time, as in,

```
C:\>backup c: a: /d:12-10-88
```

which backs up only those files changed on or after December 10, 1988.

Fifth Generation Systems Fastback and other backup products offer incremental backups, data compression, and other features, and are extremely rapid as well. Consider getting one of these products. They are well worth the expense.

As far as the number of disks used, simple arithmetic indicates that a 20 megabyte (20,000,000 byte) hard disk will require about 60 360K byte floppies for backup! A viable option is replacing a 360K floppy drive with a 720K 3.5-inch drive to reduce the number of diskettes by one-half. DOS will support both types at the same time (see "Floppy Disk, Adding").

PS/2 series owners will have a further reduction by one-half with their larger capacity drives.

Several articles I have read refer to a DEBUG utility to examine and change memory. There is a limited explanation of DEBUG commands in my Using DOS manual, but how can I obtain more information about the use of DEBUG?

The DEBUG utility not only allows you to examine and change memory, but provides a means to do limited assembly and execution of assembly language programs. It is primarily a tool for assembly-language program developers. However, it occasionally comes in very handy for the average user, as you found out.

Complete DEBUG documentation used to be included in DOS manuals. However, in DOS 4.0, DEBUG documentation was placed in the *Technical Reference Manual* for DOS. You may be able to obtain the manual from IBM, but at this time of writing it is difficult to obtain unless you are a program developer. An alternative is to use the DOS 3.3 manual, which *does* contain a full explanation of DEBUG commands. You may have to purchase this version of DOS for the DEBUG documentation if you're unable to obtain it elsewhere. The DOS 3.3 documentation of DEBUG does not explain new commands used to examine extended memory.

I get an "EOF mark not found" error message on several text files when doing a COMP (compare) operation in command prompt mode, yet the files appear to be all right. What's happening?

The end-of-file (EOF) mark is a special character (decimal 26) that marks the last byte of some files. If the EOF is missing, bytes after the end of the file may be different in two files. However, this may not be an error if the files are only processed to the last valid byte of the file. The processing program, typically a word processor, knows where the last byte of the file is without an EOF mark.

Try a COPY to duplicate the file with a new diskette, if possible. If the same error message occurs, chances are that the files *are* missing an EOF mark. If you're still uneasy about this, View each file and compare the data visually.

How do I find out how much memory there is available in my system for programs? How much is really required?

The MEM command in command prompt mode shows the bytes of total memory, the bytes available, and the largest executable program size. It also shows the amount of EMS and extended memory available and free:

```
C:\>mem
```

The /PROGRAM and /DEBUG options with MEM provide more detailed information about the content of memory, showing the actual locations and program sizes in hexadecimal. (See Figure 12.) To see this try:

```
C:\>mem /program
```

A memory size of 256K bytes is required to *install* DOS 4.0 and 360K bytes is required to operate the entire shell.

Generally, a program file (.COM or .EXE) can be loaded and executed if the memory space available is greater than the size of the program in bytes. However, most programs require additional work space and sometimes a great deal of work space, so the actual amount of extra space required varies. Many significant software packages now require at least 512K bytes to 640K bytes of total memory to run.

```
Address      Name       Size      Type
───────      ────       ────      ────
000000                  000400    Interrupt Vector
000400                  000100    ROM Communication Area
000500                  000200    DOS Communication Area

000700       IO         002140    System Program

002840       MSDOS      008E40    System Program

00B680       IO         0261D0    System Data
             ANSI       001180    DEVICE=
             DRIVER     0000E0    DEVICE=
             GMOUSE     001CA0    DEVICE=
             VDISK      0204E0    DEVICE=
                        0000C0    FILES=
                        000100    FCBS=
                        0029A0    BUFFERS=
                        000210    LASTDRIVE=
031860       MSDOS      000030    -- Free --
0318A0       CATCH      000060    Environment
031910       MSDOS      000010    -- Free --
031930       FASTOPEN   002770    Program
0340B0       COMMAND    001640    Program
035700       COMMAND    000100    Environment
035810       APPEND     001E20    Program
037640       GRAFTABL   0004A0    Program
037AF0       PRINT      0016A0    Program
0391A0       CATCH      001B30    Program
03ACE0       MEM        000070    Environment
03AD60       MSDOS      000030    -- Free --
03ADA0       SHELLB     000E80    Program
03BC30       MEM        012F00    Program
04EB40       MSDOS      0514B0    -- Free --


  655360 bytes total memory
  655360 bytes available
  410560 largest executable program size
```

Figure 12

Isn't there any way to backup just the new files
I've created? The Backup function in DOS
SHELL backs up my entire 20M byte hard disk,
and this takes a great deal of time!

To avoid backing up all of your hard disk,
use the backup options in DOS SHELL or
BACKUP in command prompt mode. There
areseveraloptions that can be used. The /M
option backs up only files that have not been
backed up previously. The /A option allows
you toa dd files to an existing backup diskette.
The /D option backs up files that have been
modified on or after a given date. Star twith the
current directory or the root directory. Some
examples of BACKUP are:

`C:\>backup /m` (backup files not previously
backed up)
`C:\>backup /m/a`   (backup and add to
existing diskette)
`C:\>backup /d:7-9-89` (backup files marked
after 7-9-89)

Another option is to use an incremental
backup in a non-DOS application program, such
as Fastback, which may be faster than the DOS
BACKUP.
A final option is to use the XCOPY command in command prompt mode. XCOPY allows many of the same options as BACKUP but

files are not held in a special format as in BACKUP diskettes. They are simply transferred as files:

```
C:\>xcopy c: a: /s /m     (files since
last BACKUP or XCOPY)
C:\>xcopy c: a: /s /d:7-9-89 (all files
since 7-9-89)
```

I keep getting the "Program to big to fit in memory" error message after installing a virtual disk. Now I can't load my word processor to change the CONFIG.SYS file for VDISK!

If you specify a virtual disk that is too large, DOS will reduce the size automatically, leaving 100K bytes of available memory after the virtual disk is installed. This is too small for many programs, hence you won't be able to load in your word processor to change the DEVICE=C:\DOS\VDISK.SYS. . . line.

Remember that the first parameter in the VDISK line is the number of kilobytes. If you specify 1024, for example, that's 1,048,576 bytes, which may be more than your available memory. The next parameter is not critical; it's the sector size of 128, 256, or 512 bytes. The next parameter is the number of entries in the virtual disk directory, also not critical. Use 64 if uncertain (maximum is 512). A typical virtual disk of 131,072 bytes is specified by:

```
DEVICE=C:\DOS\VDISK.SYS 128 512 64
```

To replace the CONFIG.SYS, use the command prompt command C:\TYPE>PRN to get a listing and then carefully enter with the change to the VDISK line. Enter by the procedure in "Files, Short ASCII." Then restart the system.

I have a single floppy drive. How can I copy a floppy diskette?

The Copy function in the DOS SHELL or the DISKCOPY command in the command prompt mode allows you to make copies with only one drive. You'll be asked to insert the "source" and the "target" diskettes at different times. Just keep in mind that the original diskette is the source diskette and that the new copy will be on the target diskette. If you're concerned about destroying the contents of the original diskette, place a write protect tab over the notch on a 5.25-inch floppy or slide the write protect switch down on a 3.5-inch diskette so that a hole is visible through the diskette.

When in the command prompt mode, specify the same drive in the DISKCOPY command:

```
C:\>diskcopy a: a:
```

I'm trying to use the SORT utility on an address file created by my word processor, but I'm not having much luck. The file is sorted improperly.

The SORT utility is designed primarily to sort text files made up of individual lines of up to hundreds of characters. Normally, there should be no non-printable characters within the line. If your word processor uses special control characters, there's a good chance that the sort will not work properly. Another problem is that some word processors do not end lines with a carriage return and line feed character.

Use the TYPE command in command prompt mode to display the file you're trying to sort. If there are odd characters such as musical notes or stars, your word processor is inserting special control characters. Use ASCII output if your word processor has that option. If each line of the file does not start on a new line of the screen in the same position, your word processor is not formatting the file lines properly for SORT. Use a new line action for each logical line.

Use /+n to define the sort column and /r to sort in reverse order; otherwise SORT will sort on column 1 in ascending (alphabetical) order. For example,

```
sort /+10 <addressa >sorteda
```

sorts file ADDRESSA on column 10 and puts the results in file SORTEDA.

What is a virtual disk and how can I use one?

A virtual disk (RAM disk) isn't a disk at all. It's system memory that is made to look like a disk. The disk is given a drive letter, can be used to store files, uses directories and subdirectories, and, in short, acts like another disk. However, whatever is on the virtual disk disappears when power is turned off!

To use a virtual disk, add two lines in your CONFIG.SYS file (see "Startup, Modifying CONFIG.SYS"), one to setup the virtual disk size and the second to change the last drive in the system to accommodate the dummy disk. Typical lines are:

```
BREAK=ON
BUFFERS=20
FILES=20
LASTDRIVE=E
DEVICE=C:\DOS\VDISK.SYS 128 512 64
. . .
```

The virtual disk in this case will be setup to have 128 kilobytes (128 x 1024 = 131,072 bytes), a sector size of 512 bytes, and 64 entries in the directory (room enough for 64 files). The LASTDRIVE parameter is changed so that drive specifier E: will be used for the virtual disk.

Since memory access is so much faster than disk access, virtual disks are excellent for files that use disk temporarily while processing files.

Glossary

Application Program — Any user program to be run. Usually a commercial piece of software such as Lotus 1-2-3 or WordPerfect, but could be a user-designed program such as a BASIC program.

AUTOEXEC.BAT — A special DOS file that performs a series of start up functions when the computer system is turned on or restarted.

Back Slash — This special symbol (\) is used to represent another level of directory in a DOS command or file path.

BASIC — A programming language included with DOS that enables a knowledgeable user to write and run his own applications.

Batch File — A sequence of DOS commands, some ordinary, some special, that can be executed automatically to perform DOS functions.

Byte — The unit used to describe the capacity of disk drives and memory. Can hold values of 0 — 255 or one character of data.

CGA (Color Graphics Adapter) — The original IBM PC color display that allows up to 640 dots by 200 dots per screen.

Command Prompt Mode — The DOS mode in which commands are entered in text form as opposed to DOS SHELL mode, in which actions are performed by visual displays and menu selection.

CONFIG.SYS — A special DOS file that defines certain system conditions. It runs when the system is turned on or restarted.

Controller — Usually a plug-in board that controls operations between the main computer system and devices such as disk drives, printers, modems, and displays.

Cursor — Any easily recognizable symbol on a display screen that marks the position on the screen. Typical cursors are underlines, vertical bars, or arrow symbols.

Directory — A list of files found on disk. There

are two types of directories: a root directory, the main directory for a disk; and a subdirectory, a lower-level directory below a root directory or another subdirectory.

DOS (Disk Operating System) — A supervisor program that oversees computer operations such as manipulating files on disk and running user programs.

DOS SHELL — An easy to use program that uses graphics displays and menus in performing DOS 4.0 functions such as listing files and directories or starting programs.

DOSSHELL.BAT — A special file used to start the DOS SHELL. Contains start up options that customize the DOS SHELL.

EDLIN — The rudimentary editor program included with DOS. Like a mini word processor.

EGA (Extended Graphics Adapter) — A medium-performance graphics display found on IBM PC series computers or compatibles that have special EGA plug-in boards.

EMS (Expanded Memory System) — A special type of memory expansion board used to add additional user memory to older IBM PC and PC-compatible systems.

Error Condition — Any of innumerable failure

conditions caused by defective electronic parts in disk drives, printers, or other devices, user operating mistakes, software programming mistakes, or system incompatibilities. Usually reported by DOS as an error message.

Escape Sequence — A special series of commands started by an Escape character and sent to a printer or other system device to perform such actions as selecting a font, bold face printing, line spacing, etc.

File — A commercial, user, or system program or data stored on disk as a single entity.

File System — A group of functions in the DOS SHELL that allows a user to manipulate disk files.

Formatting — An electronic procedure, controlled by DOS, that prepares a diskette or hard disk to store user and system files.

Group — A collection of programs displayed and manipulated in the DOS SHELL.

Hardware — The parts of a computer system made up of electronic or mechanical parts such as the keyboard, chassis, monitor, printer, plug-in boards, etc.

Hexadecimal — A special notation used to represent numbers, often used in representing computer system data.

K — 1024 of anything in computer systems. 10K bytes of memory is 10 x 1024 = 10,240 bytes.

Megabyte — 1,048,576 bytes of memory, either on disk or within the computer user memory.

Menu — Any text or graphics display in which a list of choices are displayed for user selection.

Mouse — A hand—held device that is rolled across a flat area to control the position of a cursor on a display screen. Used to "point and click" (position and select) in DOS 4.0 and other programs.

Path — A listing of the disk, directories, and file name or any portion of these in order to specify the location of a file.

PSC (Program Startup Command) — A command used to start a program from the DOS SHELL.

Read—Only — A program or data file that can be examined or displayed, but not modified or deleted.

SELECT Program — The program in DOS that builds a customized version of DOS for your system.

Software — The parts of a computer system represented by paper or programs such as documentation, files on diskette, etc.

Startup Options — Commands used in the INSTALL program or DOSSHELL.BAT file to customize the DOS SHELL to your system or needs.

Switch — An optional part of a DOS command in command prompt mode that causes the command to perform special actions. Preceded by a slash (/) in DOS commands.

System file — Either a special program with a name of the form XXXXXXXX.SYS or the file listing of all disk files obtained in the DOS SHELL.

Utilities — A group of programs in the DOS SHELL that perform disk formatting, setting time and date, and backup and restore functions. Any program that performs subordinate maintenance functions.

VGA (Virtual Graphics Interface) — A high-performance graphics display found on IBM PS/2 series computers or compatibles or on earlier computers that have added special hardware.

Index

193